CORINTHIANS
Study Guide

Search-and-Discover Bible Study Series

by John E. Baird

A Division of Standard Publishing
Cincinnati, Ohio
40016

ISBN: 0-87239-024-1

© 1975
The STANDARD PUBLISHING Company
Cincinnati, Ohio
Printed in U.S.A.

PREFACE

CORINTHIANS Study Guide, one of ten books in the Search-and-Discover Bible Study Series by Dr. John E. Baird, is devised to provide a comprehensive study of the New Testament. Through the use of both content and discussion questions in each study guide, the student has the opportunity to examine both the Bible statements and his own thoughts in order to accomplish his goal—a better understanding and a practical application of the New Testament teachings.

For the most effective use of this study guide, students are encouraged to complete the content questions at home. Read the Scripture verses for each lesson, answer the content questions, and then reread the verses in order to check the answers. This procedure reinforces learning of the material.

After completing the content questions, a student should read and contemplate the discussion questions in order to be prepared for class. Effective group discussion centering around the discussion questions presented in each chapter provides an opportunity for the expression of one's own thoughts, for the answering of questions, for an interesting exchange of ideas, and for suggestions about the application of the Scriptures in daily life.

The leader should prepare for the lesson in much the same way as the student. But also the leader must be prepared to answer questions, to offer new insights into the lesson, and to guide the students through their discussion in order to provide a significant learning experience for each individual. Leaders may find the following kinds of references helpful in preparing for the discussion: various translations of the Bible, a Bible commentary, a dictionary, a topical Bible, a concordance, an atlas, and wall maps.

Young people and adults both will find this series applicable for use in Sunday-school classes, evening study programs, vacation Bible school, camps, neighborhood Bible study groups, new member programs, and even family devotions.

—The Editor

CONTENTS

LESSON 1

1 Corinthians 1:1-31

CONTENT QUESTIONS

1. Who joined Paul in writing this letter (v. 1)? _____

_____

2. To what church was Paul writing (v. 2)? _____

3. To what additional audience was Paul writing (v. 2)? _____

_____

4. What did Paul wish for his readers (v. 3)? _____

_____

5. Why did Paul give thanks to God (v. 4)? _____

_____

6. Give two specific ways in which the Corinthians were enriched or blessed in Christ (v. 5).

    (1) _____

    (2) _____

7. What was confirmed among the Corinthian Christians (v. 6)?

_____

8. What was the status of the Corinthians in regard to spiritual gifts (v. 7)? _____

9. For what were they waiting (v. 7)? _____

_____

10. How long would Christ confirm or sustain them (v. 8)? _____

_____

11. With whom were they called into fellowship (v. 9)? _____

_____

12. What did Paul urge the Corinthians to do (v. 10)?_____

_____

13. What had Chloe's household told Paul about the Corinthians

(v. 11)?_____

14. To whom were the Corinthians giving allegiance (v. 12)?

(1)_____ (2) _____

(3)_____ (4) _____

15. List three basic questions Paul asked about these allegiances

(v. 13). (1) _____

(2) _____

(3) _____

16. Name two persons whom Paul baptized when he was in Cor-

inth (v. 14). (1)_____

(2) _____

17. Name one household or family which he baptized (v. 16). __

_____

18. What did Christ send Paul to do (v. 17)? _____

_____

19. What will God do to the wisdom of the wise (v. 19)? _____

_____

20. What has God done to the wisdom of the world (v. 20)? ____

_____

21. What people demand signs or proofs (v. 22)?_____

22. What people seek after wisdom (v. 22)? _____

23. What did Paul and his friends preach (v. 23)?_____

_____

24. How did the Jews regard this message (v. 23)? _____

25. How did the Greeks or Gentiles regard this message (v. 23)?

_____

26. How was Christ regarded by those who were called (v. 24)?

_____

27. How does God's weakness compare with men (v. 25)? _____

_____

28. How many of the Corinthian Christians would be considered wise, powerful, or noble (v. 26)? _____

29. Why did God choose the weak and foolish (vv. 27-29)?

_____

30. List four things the Christian should find in Christ Jesus, the source of life (v. 30).

    (1)_____ (2) _____

    (3)_____ (4) _____

31. Of what could the Christian boast (v. 31)? _____

DISCUSSION QUESTIONS

1. Why did Paul write this letter? Was the problem of divisions in the Corinthian church enough to cause him to write? What do you expect him to discuss in the rest of the letter? Do you feel that this problem was serious enough to receive the treatment Paul gave it? Do you think Paul was the type to get overly excited about minor matters?

2. How do you explain the contradictory view of the Corinthian Christians found in verses 2 and 11 of this chapter? Are the same people being discussed in these two verses? Can people remain saints, and call on the name of the Lord, and still quarrel? Do you think the Corinthian Christians' quarrels were serious? How bad must a quarrel become before it destroys one's relationship with God? Are disputes found among Christians today? Is our relationship to God damaged by such things? How?

3. What was Paul's real feeling about baptism? Did he consider it secondary? Would he have applied the same views to other ministers as well as himself? Why did he baptize so few persons in Corinth? What did he mean by his being thankful that he didn't baptize more? How do you explain the difference between the view of baptism presented here and Paul's view of baptism found in Romans 6:1-4?

4. Explain verse 8. How could the Corinthians be guilty of quarreling and still be guiltless or blameless? If God sustained them, why were they quarreling? In what sense does God sustain a Christian confronted by temptation?

5. What should be the attitude of the Christian toward human wisdom? Should we value the knowledge of experts? Should we value education? In what respects are knowledge and education dangerous? Is a little knowledge a dangerous thing? Why?

6. Without divine revelation and simply by his own study and thought, how much can man learn about God? Can the human race be saved by its own efforts in trying to understand God and His universe? If so, what is the purpose of our preaching "Christ crucified"? If not, why should we devote our time and money to science and knowledge?

7. Why did God ignore the powerful, the wise, the noble in His trying to reach mankind? Wouldn't He have accomplished more by turning to the best people? What did He gain by turning to the lowly and despised? Does your church try to reach the best or the despised people of your community? Do you think God approves of the way you try to go about winning people to Him? How would you characterize the lowly and despised people of your community? Who are they? Would they be accepted in your church?

8. Do people ever boast? Under what circumstances? Of what do they boast? What kind of glorying or boasting do you think Paul had in mind when he wrote this chapter? Are Christians today ever guilty of such boasting? What is the antidote for this kind of human pride?

LESSON 2

1 Corinthians 2:1-16

CONTENT QUESTIONS

1. Whose testimony had Paul proclaimed to the Corinthians (v. 1)?

_____

2. What kind of speaking did Paul avoid when he came to them (v. 1)? _____

3. What knowledge did he decide to emphasize in Corinth (v. 2)?

_____

4. What was Paul's state of mind at the time (v. 3)? _____

_____

5. If Paul's speech and preaching were not with words of wisdom, what did he have to offer his listeners (v. 4)? _____

_____

6. What was Paul's purpose in speaking in this manner (v. 5)? _

_____

7. When Paul did offer wisdom, what kind of Christians did he want to listen to him (v. 6)? _____

8. What did Paul expect to be in store for the rulers or princes of this age (v. 6)? _____

9. Whose secret wisdom was Paul imparting (v. 7)? _____

10. When had God decreed or ordained this wisdom (v. 7)? ___

_____

11. If the rulers of Paul's day had understood God's wisdom, in what way would their acts have been different (v. 8)? _____

_____

12. For whom has God prepared great things (v. 9)? _____

13. Who searches the depths of God (v. 10)? _____

14. Who really knows a man's thoughts (v. 11)? _____

15. Who comprehends the thoughts of God (v. 11)? _____

16. What Spirit had Paul received (v. 12)? _____

17. For what purpose had Paul received this Spirit (v. 12)? _____

_____

18. How did Paul impart these things and communicate this understanding (v. 13)? _____

19. Who taught him the words (v. 13)? _____

20. How does a natural or unspiritual man regard the gifts of God's Spirit (v. 14)? _____

21. Why can't such a natural man grasp spiritual things (v. 14)?

_____

22. Who is capable of judging the spiritual man (v. 15)? _____

_____

23. Who has the mind of Christ (v. 16)? _____

DISCUSSION QUESTIONS

1. Compare the first two verses of this chapter with Acts 17:16-34. Do you think Paul's experience in Athens had anything to do with his approach to the city of Corinth? Which do you think was more effective, Paul's style in Athens or Corinth? Would Paul have been more effective in Athens if he had used the Corinthian approach? Would the Corinthian Christians have been more mature, spiritually, if Paul had preached as he did in Athens? Which approach would you consider more effective in a twentieth century city?

2. What did Paul mean by saying he decided to know nothing while in Corinth except Jesus Christ crucified? What do you think Paul said in his witnessing and in his preaching? Did he say anything about Jesus except His death? Did he mention the resurrection? Did he say something about the Corinthians—their needs, their sins, their interests? In what sense, then, did Paul insist that he knew nothing but the crucifixion of Christ? What implications do you see for our Christian witness today?

3. In what sense may an individual's faith rest on the wisdom of men rather than on the power of God? Do you know people with faith like this? What are they lacking? Do you think they can develop a more spiritually powerful faith? How? What do you think will happen to people who have a faith resting only on the wisdom of men?

4. How can Christians deal with social issues if they know only the crucified Christ? Does the crucifixion of Christ have social implications? What? If we were really to witness to our faith in Christ and in the power of God, what would we say about social problems? What form would our social message take?

5. In this chapter Paul wrote about one's having the Spirit of God, understanding the gifts bestowed upon us by God, and having the mind of Christ. Did he refer only to himself or to all Christians? Is the ability to impart truths in spiritual language limited to Paul, to the apostles, to ministers? How can we tell whether one teaches by the Spirit of God, or whether he merely claims to speak for the Spirit of God? Certainly, not all Christian teachers agree. How can we know which teaching is inspired?

6. Explain the term spiritual person. How can we identify such a person? How does one become a spiritual person? On the basis of verse 15, what powers and privileges does such a person have? In what sense does the spiritual person judge all things?

7. Paul indicated that if the rulers of the day had understood God's plan, they would not have crucified Christ. Does this claim mean that our salvation rests upon the sin and disobedience of these rulers? What do you think God would have done if the Romans had eliminated the death penalty and refused to crucify our Lord? Was His death really necessary? Would it not have been adequate for Him to show us the spirit of sacrifice, without actually dying?

LESSON 3

1 Corinthians 3:1-23

CONTENT QUESTIONS

1. On what level did Paul think of his readers of this letter (v. 1)? _____

2. How had he fed them, spiritually, when he was with them (v. 2)? _____

3. What spiritual diet did he consider them currently able to digest (v. 2)? _____

4. What evidence did Paul offer of their immaturity (v. 3)? _____

_____

5. How did they behave (v. 3)? _____

6. What was the evidence of this level of behavior (v. 4)? _____

_____

7. What status did Paul claim for himself as a result of his labors in Corinth (v. 5)? _____

8. What had Apollos contributed in Corinth (v. 6)? _____

_____

9. Who was really responsible for the growth of Christianity in Corinth (v. 6)? _____

10. Who is most important in this growth process (v. 7)? _____

11. Who is superior, the one who plants or the one who waters (v. 8)? _____

12. What is the basis for man's wages or reward (v. 8)? _____

13. How did Paul refer to the Corinthian Christians (v. 9)? _____

_____

14. What had Paul done, as a builder (v. 10)? _____

_____

15. Who is the Foundation of the building (v. 11)? _____

16. List some possible building materials (v. 12). _____

_____

17. What element will test the building (v. 13)? _____

18. What happens to the man whose building survives (v. 14)? __

_____

19. What happens to the man whose building is destroyed (v. 15)?

_____

20. What kind of building were the Corinthians (v. 16)? _____

_____

21. Who occupied this building (v. 16)? _____

22. What happens to one who defiles or destroys God's temple
    (v. 17)? _____

23. How may one become wise (v. 18)? _____

24. How does God regard the wisdom of this world (v. 19)? _____

_____

25. How does God take the wise of this world (v. 19)? _____

_____

26. What does God know about the thoughts or ideas of the wise
    (v. 20)? _____

27. Of what should no one boast or glory (v. 21)? _____

28. What did the Corinthian Christians possess (v. 22)? _____

_____

29. To whom did the Corinthian Christians belong (v. 23)? _____

DISCUSSION QUESTIONS

1. How can you identify an immature Christian? Is the term babe in Christ related to physical age? To length of time since one accepted Christ? Paul affirmed that jealousy and strife are two indications of immaturity. What other marks would you include? How would you classify yourself on the scale of Christian maturity? As a babe? A child? A teenager? A young adult? A mature Christian? Is Christian maturity different from other types of maturity, or are all marks of maturity basically the same?

2. How do you feel about the respect which Christians should have for their ministers? To what extent should a Christian be proud of the fine qualities of his minister? How do we avoid falling into a my-minister-is-greater-than-your-minister kind of pride?

3. Since God gives the growth to Christians, what is the Christian's own responsibility? Is there anything we should do? How does God produce this growth? What can we do for ourselves? What does the minister do for us in planting and watering?

4. In what sense is Christ the foundation of the church? Compare verse 11 of this chapter with Matthew 16:18. What did Jesus mean by this rock?

5. How does a Christian minister or teacher build on Christ? What would you classify as gold, silver, precious stones? What would you classify as wood, hay, stubble? In what respect does an individual Christian incorporate these things into his own life? What would you consider the gold, silver, precious stones, wood, hay, or stubble in building individual Christian character?

6. Does the term God's temple refer to individuals or to the entire church in Corinth? In what way may one destroy the temple? In what way can one destroy the church? Why would God permit the destruction of a temple belonging to Him?

7. In what sense would everything belong to the Christians in Corinth? How would the earlier preachers belong to them? After all, wasn't their faith produced by this preaching? Then wouldn't they belong to the preachers, rather than vice versa? In what sense would life and death, the present and the future, belong to them?

LESSON 4

1 Corinthians 4:1-21

CONTENT QUESTIONS

1. How did Paul want the Corinthians to regard him (v. 1)?____

   _____

2. What was required of such servants (v. 2)? _____

   _____

3. How did Paul feel about his being judged by the Corinthians

   (v. 3)? _____

4. Whom did Paul regard as his real Judge (v. 4)? _____

5. What will the Lord do when He comes (v. 5)? _____

   _____

6. What will every man receive from God at that time (v. 5)?

   _____

7. To whom was Paul applying all of these considerations (v. 6)?

   _____ and _____

8. For whose benefit was Paul writing (v. 6)?_____

9. What change did Paul hope to see produced in the lives of the

   Corinthians (v. 6)? _____

   _____

10. How did the Corinthians happen to have everything they pos-

    sessed (v. 7)?_____

11. What reason did Paul give for wishing the Corinthians might

    reign as kings (v. 8)? _____

12. To whom had the apostles become a spectacle (v. 9)? _____

_____

13. List three ways in which Paul compared himself and the other apostles with the Corinthian Christians (v. 10).

We are _____ ; you are _____

We are _____ ; you are _____

We are _____ ; you are _____

14. How were the apostles getting along (v. 11)? _____

_____

15. How did the apostles react to their problems (vv. 12, 13)? __

_____

16. What status did the apostles hold in the world (v. 13)? _____

_____

17. Why did Paul write these things to the Corinthian Christians (v. 14)?_____

18. In what sense was Paul their father (v. 15)? _____

_____

19. How did Paul want them to react to him (v. 16)? _____

_____

20. Why had Paul sent Timothy to them (v. 17)? _____

_____

21. Who did not anticipate Paul's return to Corinth (v. 18)? _____

_____

22. What did Paul expect to find out when he returned (v. 19)? _

_____

23. What is the essence of the kingdom of God (v. 20)?_____

_____

24. What alternatives did Paul give the Corinthians in regard to

his return to Corinth (v. 21)? _____

_____

DISCUSSION QUESTIONS

1. What is your reaction to your having God as your judge? Paul seemed to feel that God will finally commend all men (v. 5). Do you really think he meant all, or was he talking about a limited group? Will God finally commend all men no matter what kind of life each led? What commendation may we expect? Do you feel that you have any claim upon God's commendation? What?

2. What did Paul mean by the Corinthians' learning to live according to the Scriptures (v. 6)? What Scripture do you think he had in mind? What passages would particularly apply to the Corinthians as revealed in the letter thus far? What Scripture would we have that they didn't have? Which Scripture do you feel is most needed by the average members of your church?

3. Paul apparently felt that the hardships of an apostle's life implied a judgment upon the ease and prosperity of the Corinthian Christians. Do you feel that Christians today have life as difficult as did the apostles? If not, does our modern prosperity represent a judgment upon us? Would Paul feel that we have things too easy? In what way? If we were the kind of Christians that the apostles were, what would our lives be like?

4. Paul asked the Corinthians to be his imitators (v. 16). Was he wise in doing this? In seeking to live the Christian life should we ever imitate anyone besides Jesus Christ? Who? How can we avoid the sins of others if we seek to imitate others? Should parents encourage their children to imitate them? In what respects would young Christians be safe in imitating you? What would you prefer to have them avoid?

5. What did Paul mean by the statement the kingdom of God is not in word, but in power (v. 20)? When is talk without power? What gives genuine power to one's language? If one had to choose between words and deeds, which would be more important? Why? Would you say that your church places emphasis on talk or on power? Which is characteristic of your own Christian life?

LESSON 5

1 Corinthians 5:1-13

CONTENT QUESTIONS

1. What report had Paul heard about the Corinthians (v. 1)? ___

   _____

2. How serious was the sin (v. 1)? _____

   _____

3. What was the nature of the sin (v. 1)? _____

   _____

4. What did Paul feel should have been the reaction of the Corinthian Christians to this sin (v. 2)?_____

5. What did Paul feel should have been done with the guilty person (v. 2)? _____

6. In what sense was Paul present in Corinth (v. 3)? _____

7. On whose authority did Paul rely in approaching judgment on
   this case (v. 4)? _____

8. Under what circumstances were the Corinthians to take action
   (v. 4)?_____

9. What were the Corinthians to do with the guilty person (v. 5)?

   _____

10. What was to be the motive for their actions (v. 5)?_____

    _____

11. How did Paul feel about the boasting of the Corinthians (v. 6)?

    _____

12. What illustration did Paul use to help the Corinthians grasp the extent of their problem (v. 6)? _____

_____

13. In keeping with this illustration, what did Paul instruct them to do (v. 7)? _____

14. What sacrifice was the basis for these instructions (v. 7)?

_____

15. Name two things represented by leaven in Paul's illustration (v. 8). _____ and _____

16. What two things did the unleavened bread represent (v. 8)?

_____ and _____

17. What previous instructions had Paul given the Corinthians (v. 9)? _____

18. Why didn't Paul intend for the Corinthian Christians to separate themselves completely from all the sinful people of the world (v. 10)? _____

_____

19. With what kind of wicked people should they refuse to associate (v. 11)? _____

20. List the six sins Paul mentioned (v. 11).

(1) _____ (2) _____

(3) _____ (4) _____

(5) _____ (6) _____

21. To what extent should Christians go in separating themselves from wicked people (v. 11)? _____

22. How did Paul feel about his apostolic authority over persons outside the church (v. 12)? _____

23. Whom were the Christians to judge (v. 12)? _____

21

24. Who would judge those on the outside (v. 13)? _____

_____

DISCUSSION QUESTIONS

1. What do you think of the moral standards Paul taught the early Christians? Was anything wrong in the relationship between a man and his stepmother? Why would the action be wrong if they loved each other and nobody else was hurt? If Paul's standards were appropriate for the first century, how strictly do you think they can be applied today?

2. What is the responsibility of the church and its officers in disciplining Christians? What right does a Christian or group of Christians have to apply punishment upon other Christians? What right did Paul have to pronounce judgment without a hearing? What is to prevent Christians from attacking each other over personal quarrels or disagreements? How do you harmonize Paul's commands in verse 12 with Jesus' command in Matthew 7:1?

3. How far should Christians go in the "destruction of the flesh, that the spirit may be saved" (v. 5)? If the offender had not repented, following the withdrawal of fellowship, what else do you think Paul would have recommended? If the church has political power, should it use this power in the discipline of its members? If the tortures of the Inquisition, a former Roman Catholic tribunal for the destruction and punishment of heresy, were wrong, where should Christians draw the line? In their zeal to defend the faith and reclaim those who have fallen away into sin, what is to prevent the Christians from sinning?

4. In what way, if any, should Christians limit their associations with people of the world? In what way should we withdraw from fellow Christians who have fallen into sin? Should we treat fellow Christians worse than non-Christians? If not, how do you explain Paul's commands in verses 9-11? If so, then what is the meaning of the brotherhood we have in Christ? Are Christians required to break the relationship between themselves and their fellows who have fallen into sin? Isn't the Christian expected to assist his fallen brother? What steps do you think Paul would have recommended? What steps would you recommend in similar cases today?

22

5. What do you think of the list of sins given in verse 11? Did Paul include enough? Should other sins be on the list? Did Paul include things considered sins which should not be included? Have attitudes about these sins changed during the past two thousand years?

6. How do you understand the difference in Paul's treatments of the divisions in the Corinthian church and of this case of immoral conduct? Which sin did Paul regard as the worst? How do you explain the long address Paul gave to the church divisions in comparison to this brief and almost abrupt speech on the case of immorality? Which problem do you think is more acute in the church today, immorality or internal strife? Do you see variations here in regard to the section of the country concerned? The age group of the Christians? The culture in which the church exists?

7. What did Paul mean by his not judging outsiders? If we don't judge non-Christians in some respect, what motivation is there for the Christian witness? Why should we bother with other people unless we judge them to be lost and in need of the Savior? If we are concerned about this need, aren't we thereby judging persons?

LESSON 6

1 Corinthians 6:1-20

CONTENT QUESTIONS

1. What were the Corinthian Christians doing when they had a grievance against another (v. 1)? _____

   _____

2. What evidence of the competence of the saints as judges did Paul offer (v. 2)? _____

3. Who, in addition to the world, will the saints judge (v. 3)?

   _____

4. Before whom were the Corinthians placing their disputes (v. 4)? _____

5. How did Paul want the Corinthians to feel (v. 5)? _____

6. What difficult question did Paul raise about their conduct (v. 5)? _____

7. What were the Corinthian Christians actually doing in their disputes (v. 6)? _____

8. How did Paul feel about lawsuits among Christians (v. 7)?

   _____

9. What alternatives did Paul consider preferable to lawsuits (v. 7)? (1) _____

    (2) _____

10. Instead, what did the Corinthians do (v. 8)? _____

    _____

24

11. Whom did they victimize (v. 8)? _____

12. Who will not inherit the kingdom of God (v. 9)? _____

13. List ten sins Paul felt served to classify one as unrighteous (vv. 9, 10). (1) _____ (2) _____

    (3) _____ (4) _____

    (5) _____ (6) _____

    (7) _____ (8) _____

    (9) _____ (10) _____

14. What kind of people had the Corinthians been before conversion (v. 11)? _____

15. What had happened to them when they became Christians (v. 11) ? _____

16. On what authority had this change taken place (v. 11)? _____

    _____

17. While Paul believed that all things were lawful for the Christian, he also gave two qualifying principles. What were they (v. 12)? (1) _____

    (2) _____

18. What will happen to both the food and the stomach (v. 13)?

    _____

19. For whom is the body meant (v. 13)? _____

20. What proof did Paul offer for his belief that God will finally raise us up (v. 14)? _____

21. What is the relationship of a Christian's body to Christ (v. 15)? _____

22. How did Paul feel about prostitution (v. 15)? _____

    _____

23. What happens to one who joins himself to a prostitute (v. 16)?

_____

24. What happens to one united to the Lord (v. 17)?_____

_____

25. Against what does the immoral man sin (v. 18)?_____

26. What is the Christian's body (v. 19)?_____

_____

27. Why isn't the Christian his own boss (v. 20)? _____

_____

DISCUSSION QUESTIONS

1. How do you think Paul would have recommended handling disagreements within the church membership? Would he ever have sanctioned Christians' going to court? Do you think he would have set up some form of church court? How would he have done it? In view of verse 7, would Paul have favored any kind of dispute-solving mechanism? How do you think he would have handled this problem under the American system of justice?

2. What did Paul mean by saying the saints will judge the world and angels? Isn't God the judge? How can Christians function as judges? Will saints actually decide cases or will they merely serve as examples of how life should be lived? But if saints are merely to be examples, how would this qualify them to decide disputes?

3. Do you agree with Paul that it is better to suffer wrong than to have a lawsuit? Wouldn't this way of living simply make Christians the victims of all society? How can one stand up for the right while accepting wrong and putting up with injustice? Do these same principles apply to rearing children? Is it better to teach them to be meek and to accept whatever comes, or should we teach them to stand up for their rights?

4. What do you think about Paul's including the sin of homosexuality in his list of those who will not inherit the kingdom of God? Is homosexuality a sin? Does a person have any choice about being a homosexual? Is this something that might have been a

sin in the culture of Paul's day but not in other times and places? What is your opinion about the matter in our day? How should the church minister to homosexuals?

5. To what extent should the laws of the land reflect the moral standards of the Christian? Do we have any right to legislate the behavior of others who may not accept the Christian way of life? On the other hand, if we do not embody our standards in legislation, how can we hope to bring up our children to live by Christian standards? Which kinds of behavior should the law attempt to control and which are outside the concern of the law?

6. How do you feel about the sin of prostitution? Read Genesis 38:15-19. Was Paul stating an eternal principle when he condemned prostitution, or was he merely talking in his own time and culture? What stand should Christians today take on this matter? What do you think of the argument that areas for legalized prostitution would help authorities control disease and keep the streets safe after dark? If the Christian agrees with Paul and shuns this form of immorality, does he then have any right to legislate against this kind of behavior, thus forcing his moral standards upon non-Christians?

7. What did Paul mean about the Christian's being bought with a price? What was the price? To whom was it paid? From whom were we purchased? What are the implications of this idea? Is there any possibility that we can be free if someone has purchased us? If freedom is an illusion, is it wrong for a Christian to keep seeking to be free? Should a Christian work for political freedom? For economic freedom?

8. How can we glorify God in our bodies? How does this principle relate to what we eat? What we drink? What we wear? Can a Christian follow this principle and wear jewelry? Use cosmetics? When does one's concern for the health and welfare of his body cease to be a glorification of God and become a form of idolatry, a glorification of the body for its own sake? How can a Christian glorify God in his body if he happens to be ill? If he has some physical handicap? How important is good care for the body? Should one get up early to pray if early rising means he must lose sleep? Should one ever starve himself in order to feed someone else who is hungry? Read 2 Corinthians 11:23-27. Was Paul a good example of glorifying God in his body?

27

LESSON 7

1 Corinthians 7:1-40

CONTENT QUESTIONS

1. What caused Paul to discuss the various subjects in this chapter (v. 1)? _____

2. What reason did Paul give to recommend marriage (v. 2)? ___
_____

3. Who rules the body of a wife (v. 4)? _____

4. Who rules the body of a husband (v. 4)? _____

5. What did Paul think could constitute an acceptable reason for temporarily avoiding sex in marriage (v. 5)? _____

6. What did Paul wish for his readers (v. 7)? _____

7. What advice did he have for the unmarried and the widows (v. 8)? _____

8. What authority did Paul claim for his advice to married people (v. 10)? _____

9. What did Paul advise for a man with a non-Christian wife (v. 12)? _____

10. What did he advise for a woman with a non-Christian husband (v. 13)? _____

11. What kind of home atmosphere is in accord with God's will and calling (v. 15)? _____

12. What should be the objective of a Christian who is married to

a non-Christian (v. 16)? _____

13. What really counts in a Christian's daily life (v. 19)? _____

_____

14. How should a servant or slave, who becomes a Christian, feel about his condition of slavery (v. 21)? _____

15. Why should a Christian not become a slave of men (v. 23)? _

_____

16. What authority did Paul have for his commands to the unmarried(v. 25)? _____

17. What reason did Paul give for recommending that single people remain single (v. 26)? _____

18. What did Paul predict for those who disagreed and married (v. 28)? _____

19. List five human actions or concerns which should not involve the Corinthian Christians because of the radical changes about to take place in their lives (vv. 29-31).

    (1) _____

    (2) _____

    (3) _____

    (4) _____

    (5) _____

20. What was one of Paul's main desires for the Corinthians (v. 32)? _____

21. What would probably be the chief concern of a married man (v. 33)? _____

22. What would probably be the chief concern of a married woman (v. 34)? _____

23. What positive goal did Paul have in mind in writing this advice (v. 35)? _____

24. Under what condition may a widowed Christian marry whomever she pleases (v. 39)? _____

25. How would a widow be happiest (v. 40)? _____

_____

26. What was his authority in taking this position (v. 40)? _____

_____

DISCUSSION QUESTIONS

1. Paul apparently wrote this chapter to respond to some specific questions sent him by the Corinthian Christians. What do you think the questions were? Which of these questions still trouble Christians today? If the members of your church could ask one question of the apostle Paul today, would they ask one of these questions? If not, what would they ask? If you could personally ask one question of the apostle today, what would it be?

2. What do you think of Paul's comments in verses 12 and 25 that he had no command of the Lord on these problems? If he had no command of the Lord, what right did he have to offer his own advice? Do Christians today have this same authority to offer advice to their fellow Christians? What about teachers, ministers, officers in the church? How do you think the Corinthians would have reacted to this advice on Paul's personal authority, particularly those who belonged to the Apollos, Cephas, or Christ parties (1 Corinthians 1:12)? Do you think admissions of his lack of a command from God make Paul more or less trustworthy to his readers, in that time or in this?

3. Paul seemed to take the position that the ideal state for a Christian man or woman would be to remain single. What arguments did he advance, in this chapter, for such a conclusion? How would you reconcile Paul's position with the principle stated in Genesis 2:18? Which would be preferable in our time and culture, for a Christian to be single or married? What about ministers and other specialized Christian workers? Should they marry?

4. In what sense can a Christian wife consecrate an unbelieving husband and cause the children to be holy (v. 14)? Did Paul imply that one person can be saved by the faith of another? If not, how does this consecration take place? Is the Christian partner in the marriage responsible for doing anything to consecrate the non-Christian partner and to sanctify the children? If so, what?

5. Paul implied that any Christian married to a non-Christian should not seek a divorce (vv. 12, 13). How far should the Christian go in following this rule and seeking to preserve the marriage? If the non-Christian partner makes church attendance difficult or objects to the Christian's participating in church activities, should the marriage be maintained? What should the Christian do if the partner deliberately turns the children away from Christianity? At what point does the Christian stop trying to convert the unbeliever and consider separation or divorce?

6. What do you think of Paul's command that a widow is free to marry in the Lord? Does the command imply that one is not free to marry outside the Lord? Read 2 Corinthians 6:14-15. Would this advice apply to our day as well as to Paul's day? With various denominations and beliefs, how can one know who is really an unbeliever? How can parents teach this principle to their children without seeming to be old-fashioned, prejudiced, and narrow-minded? How can the contemporary congregation teach this principle to its members? How far should a young person go in social contacts with non-Christians? Should a Christian ever date a non-Christian?

7. What is the relationship between a Christian's moral principles and his emotional life? Notice verses 5, 9, 36, and 37. Was Paul implying that a Christian would still be troubled by passions? Isn't one's Christianity supposed to free him from this kind of thing? Why did Paul imply that one should give in to his passions? Why shouldn't the Christian be commanded to master his feelings, exercise perfect self-control, and remain pure and sinless at all times? If Christians have problems, what responsibilities do we have toward helping one another? What can we do to strengthen husband or wife, children, young people, other Christians?

LESSON 8

1 Corinthians 8:1-13

CONTENT QUESTIONS

1. What general topic concerned Paul (v. 1)? _____

   _____

2. How do love and knowledge differ (v. 1)? _____

   _____

3. If a person thinks he knows something, how wise is he (v. 2)?

   _____

4. What is true of those who love God (v. 3)? _____

5. What did a Christian know about idols (v. 4)? _____

   _____

6. How many gods will a Christian accept (v. 4)? _____

7. How many gods or lords had followers in Paul's day (v. 5)? _

   _____

8. Where might these gods be found (v. 5)? _____

   _____

9. In what God did a Christian believe (v. 6)? _____

   _____

10. What two aspects of God, the Father, did Paul list (v. 6)?

    (1) _____

    (2) _____

11. In what Lord did a Christian believe (v. 6)? _____

12. What two aspects of this Lord did Paul list (v. 6)?

(1) _____

(2) _____

13. Were all Christians certain about the unreality of idols (v. 7)?

_____

14. If one had been accustomed to idol sacrifices, how might he feel about eating certain food (v. 7)? _____

15. What would these feelings do to his conscience (v. 7)? _____

16. In reality, what would eating or not eating various food do to a Christian's relationship to God (v. 8)? _____

17. What was the danger in the liberty that Christians enjoyed in this regard (v. 9)? _____

18. What might have been the reaction in an observer who saw a Christian eating in an idol's temple (v. 10)? _____

_____

19. What could have been the result, if the observer happened to be a weak Christian (v. 11)? _____

20. How did Paul characterize this weak individual so as to make the Corinthians think twice about hurting him (v. 11)? _____

21. If you injure another person, against whom do you sin (v. 12)?

(1)_____ (2) _____

22. If food is going to cause a brother to fall, what rule of living should the Christian adopt (v. 13)? _____

DISCUSSION QUESTIONS

1. In regard to the worship of idols, is the average person today much different from people in Paul's day? What idols do we worship in our time and culture? (Note: To worship means literally "to give worth to," to give worth-ship or to assign ultimate value.) What is the evidence that we worship idols?

2. Is any form of idol worship a danger to Christians today? Can a Christian offend a weaker brother by appearing to participate in some form of idol worship, or is the basic problem discussed in this chapter one that does no longer exist? What places or activities would you list which Christians should avoid because of fear of misleading their Christian brethren?

3. What do you think of Paul's principle that our acts should be controlled by our concern about the way others will react to us? Should we not determine right and wrong for ourselves, in terms of our relationship to God, without worrying about how others feel? How can we draw the line between those times when we should be concerned about the opinions of others and those times when we should rely solely upon our own conscience?

4. What do you think about our permitting the weakest persons in the Christian faith to determine standards of behavior? Isn't this being unfair to strong, mature Christians? Isn't it also being unfair to the weak? How can they become strong if the others always cater to them? When should we act in such a way to spare the feelings of the weak? When should we act to enable them to become more mature?

5. The effort to avoid offending weak Christian brethren does little to help them in a positive sense. How would you have advised the Corinthian Christians to treat their weaker brethren in order to overcome these old feelings about idols? What should we do in the church today to develop mature Christians? Is it ever necessary to offend the weak in order to help them grow up? Under what circumstances?

6. How do you feel about regarding all other Christians as brothers for whom Christ died (v. 11)? Can you really feel this way about your fellow Christians without regard to class, race, nationality, age? Which barrier is the most difficult for you to overcome as you meet other Christians? What differences would there be in our behavior as Christians if we could succeed in treating one another as brothers for whom Christ died? What can we do to get Christians to feel this way about one another?

LESSON 9

1 Corinthians 9:1-27

CONTENT QUESTIONS

1. What four marks of his authority did Paul list for the Corinthians (v. 1)? (1) _____

   (2) _____

   (3) _____

   (4) _____

2. What was the seal or proof of his apostleship (v. 2)? _____

   _____

3. To whom was Paul defending himself (v. 3)? _____

4. List two basic rights Paul claimed for his own (vv. 4, 5).

   (1) _____

   (2) _____

5. What individuals or groups of early church leaders were married (v. 5)? (1) _____

   (2) _____

6. List one additional right Paul claimed for himself and Barnabas, but which his critics denied him (v. 6). _____

7. List three occupations Paul claimed to be parallel to his own in some respects (v. 7). (1) _____

   (2) _____

   (3) _____

8. What other authority could Paul cite in support of his position that he had a right to be supported (v. 8)? _____

9. What Mosaic command did Paul quote (v. 9)? _____

_____

10. With what feeling do plowmen plow and threshers thresh (v. 10)? _____

11. What had Paul done that he felt he could claim material benefits from the Corinthians (v. 11)? _____

_____

12. Why hadn't Paul attempted to enforce this claim on the Corinthians (v. 12)? _____

13. Who could claim support from the offerings of religious people (v. 13)? _____

14. What had the Lord commanded about the support of ministers (v. 14)? _____

15. What reason did Paul give for his not demanding a salary from the Corinthians (v. 15)? _____

16. Why couldn't Paul boast about the preaching he had done (v. 16)? _____

17. What was Paul's reward for preaching (v. 18)? _____

_____

18. Why had Paul become a servant or slave to all men (v. 19)?

_____

19. Why had Paul emphasized his being a Jew and placed himself under the law (v. 20)? _____

20. Why had Paul also placed himself outside the law (v. 21)? __

_____

21. What law, then, was Paul really under (v. 21)? _____

22. What was Paul doing to help to save some people (v. 22)? __

23. For what reason had he done all this (v. 23)? _____

24. In what respect is a Christian like a runner (v. 24)? _____

25. Why should a Christian, like a runner, be temperate or exercise self-control in all things (v. 25)?_____

26. Why did he struggle to keep his body disciplined and subdued (v. 27)? _____

DISCUSSION QUESTIONS

1. Are Christians obligated to preach the gospel? Or, was this obligation just a personal commitment felt by Paul and the apostles? Are various people obligated to preach in different ways? What form of preaching do you think is most effective in our day? What form do you find easiest for you?

2. Was Paul right in making the gospel free of charge to the Corinthians? Would they have taken the message more seriously if he had laid more demands upon them? How should we appeal to people today? Should we emphasize the benefits and blessings of Christianity, or should we emphasize difficulties and challenges? Do we drive people away when we emphasize the requirements of full commitment to Christ? Are we in danger of making insincere Christians when we try to make Christianity too appealing?

3. What gives a minister his standing in a congregation? Would he lose status if he refused to accept a salary as Paul did? Do we expect too much of a minister if we ask him to earn his status solely by what he does and says?

4. From what you know of Paul, what grounds for boasting would you say he had? List some of the things of which he could have been proud. Which would apply to his life before he became a Christian? Which would apply to his life after he became a Christian? Which ones do you feel are most admirable? Would

any of these things excite admiration today? Among Christians? Among people in general? Are Christian standards of what is worth boasting about significantly different from the values of the general public? How? What would you say, personally, is the accomplishment of which you are most proud in your own life?

5. How necessary is it for a Christian to work for a living? Are ministers and missionaries the only ones who should expect others to support them? What about persons on welfare? What about retired persons or those who draw disability? Do they have a right, as Christians, to accept support or should they find some sort of gainful employment? Does society have a Christian responsibility to provide help for those who do not or cannot work? If so, what form should such help take? Should Christians permit their brethren to accept help from the government? Is it the duty of the church to take care of the Christian needy?

6. To what extent do the financial requirements of Christianity put obstacles in the way of the gospel (see v. 12)? Would people in Corinth have been offended if Paul had demanded support? Do you know of people today who are kept away from Christ because "the church is always asking for money"? Is this a genuine reason or merely an excuse? What right does the church have to ask Christians for money? Would the church be more effective if it did not do so?

7. Must the Christian be a hypocrite in order to be an effective witness of his Christianity? Was Paul being hypocritical when he acted in the way recorded in verses 19-23? Compare Galatians 2:11-14. Are there times when we should not be genuine and forthright? Are there times when we should avoid telling the complete and absolute truth? If so, what kind of standards of truth and sincerity do we have? If not, how can we avoid offending people and thereby driving them away from Christ? Doesn't the "end" of saving people justify the "means" by which we accomplish the task?

8. What did Paul mean about being rejected or disqualified (v. 27)? Would he actually have been lost? Compare John 10:27-29. See also Hebrews 10:26, 27. Did Paul merely mean he would have been disqualified as an apostle or as a preacher? In what sense today may Christians be disqualified? What happens to them if they are?

LESSON 10

1 Corinthians 10:1-33

CONTENT QUESTIONS

1. What five facts about their ancestors did Paul want the Corinthians to know (vv. 1-4)? (1) _____

    (2) _____

    (3) _____

    (4) _____

    (5) _____

2. Whom did that rock represent (v. 4)? _____

3. What was the evidence that God was not pleased with them

    (v. 5)? _____

4. What should this history have signified to the Corinthians (v.

    6)? _____

5. Give four specific sins Paul warned the Corinthians to avoid

    (vv. 7-10). (1) _____

    (2) _____

    (3) _____

    (4) _____

6. Why was this history written (v. 11)? _____

    _____

7. How should one react when he feels that he is standing well

    (v. 12)? _____

8. When we are tempted, what can we expect God to do (v. 13)?

_____

_____

9. What did Paul beg the Corinthians to do about the worship of idols (v. 14)? _____

10. What did Paul consider to be the real meaning of the cup of blessing (v. 16)? _____

11. What did he consider to be the real meaning of the communion bread (v. 16)? _____

12. They partake from how many loaves of bread (v. 17)? _____

13. What did the practice of Israel in regard to eating sacrifices prove about the worshipers (v. 18)? _____

14. To whom did the pagans actually sacrifice (v. 20)? _____

15. What final instructions did Paul give about partaking of communion and then also participating in idol worship (v. 21)?

_____

_____

16. Give two qualifications or objections that Paul raised with those who insisted that all things were lawful for the Christian (v. 23). (1) _____

    (2) _____

17. How should a Christian treat his neighbor (v. 24)? _____

_____

18. How should a Christian feel about eating food sold in the marketplace (v. 25)?_____

19. What principle should govern a Christian housewife in doing her grocery shopping (v. 26)? _____

_____

20. How should a Christian, invited out to dinner, feel about the food placed before him (v. 27)? _____

21. Under what conditions should a Christian refuse to eat food placed before him (vv. 28, 29)? _____

22. In what mood should a Christian eat (v. 30)? _____

23. To what purpose should a Christian eat—or do anything else (v. 31)? _____

24. List three groups that Paul tried not to offend (v. 32).

    (1) _____

    (2) _____

    (3) _____

25. What was Paul's purpose in seeking to avoid offense (v. 33)?

    _____

DISCUSSION QUESTIONS

1. Why don't people pay more attention to God when He does so much for them? What caused the Israelites to rebel against God, after He, through Moses, had given them deliverance from slavery and the food and drink they needed? Why did they continue to desire evil? Are we any better than they? What causes some of us to turn against God?

2. Paul listed at least four sins of the Israelites: idolatry, immorality, testing the Lord, and grumbling. Which of these is most serious? Which is most basic? Does one of these lead to another, and if so, in what way? To what extent were the Corinthians indulging in these sins? To what extent do we, today, exhibit such sins? (Read Numbers 25:1-9; Exodus 32:6-10; and Numbers 21:6-9.)

3. Why is it that the one who thinks he stands is most in danger of falling (v. 12)? Isn't one aware of the danger before that danger comes upon him? Doesn't it help one's Christian life to be confident that sin has been overcome? How can we have any joy as Christians if we are always afraid that we are going to sin and be punished for it? What can we do in order to take heed and avoid falling?

4. If God always provides a way of escape when we are tempted (v. 13), why do Christians sin so much? Do we fail because of our own weakness or because the devil makes us do it? Have you ever found yourself in a situation where everything you could possibly do or say would be wrong? Where is the way of escape which God provides in cases like this?

5. In what sense is participation in the communion service a participation in the body of Christ? Does that participation lie in the bread, in the company of Christians, or in a mystical union between each Christian and God? Does the participation lie in one of these, all of these, or in something else? In what ways is the communion service similar to the sacrifices of Israel? In what ways is it different?

6. Is it true that all things are lawful for the Christian? What about those things that are against the laws of his state or his nation? When Paul raised questions about what was helpful and what was constructive, wasn't he putting into effect another set of laws? How do these guidelines differ from such Old Testament laws as the Ten Commandments? Don't we as Christians have to have rules to go by, especially in modern times?

7. Under what circumstances should we be guided by the conscience of other people? How do you understand verse 29? When do we follow the principle of refusing to do something for the sake of another person's conscience (see vv. 32, 33)? When do we follow the liberty we enjoy in Christ without being concerned about another person's scruples (see v. 30)? How do we know what is best to do with regard to the problems and temptations of our day?

8. When do we, as Christians, have a right to raise questions and objections about the behavior of brethren in Christ? Can we ever demand that another Christian stop exercising his liberty in a way that is offensive to us? If a Christian is giving thanks for his food and drink, should we denounce him for what he is eating and drinking? Read 1 Corinthians 5:11, 12. How could Paul give commands like this in chapter 5 and then talk about Christian liberty in 10:29? Was Paul guilty of trying to determine, on the basis of his own scruples, what Christian liberty should be for the people in Corinth?

LESSON 11

1 Corinthians 11:1-34

CONTENT QUESTIONS

1. Whom did Paul imitate (v. 1)? _____

2. Give two reasons why Paul praised and complimented the Corinthians (v. 2). (1) _____

   (2) _____

3. Who is the head of every man (v. 3)? _____

4. Who is the head of the woman (v. 3)? _____

5. If a man prayed with his hat on, what did he do (v. 4)? _____

   _____

6. If a woman prayed without a hat or veil, what did she do (v. 5)? _____

7. How did Paul feel about a woman's having her head shaved (v. 6)? _____

8. Why did Paul regard the woman as the glory of the man (vv. 7, 8)? _____

9. What reasons did Paul give for the interdependence of men and women (v. 12)? (1) _____

   (2) _____

10. What did Paul feel that nature revealed about hair length for men (v. 14)? _____

11. About hair length for woman (v. 15)? _____

12. What did Paul say resulted when the Christians in Corinth got together (v. 17)? _____

13. Give one specific criticism Paul directed against their assemblies (v. 18). _____

14. What did Paul say it was impossible for them to eat (v. 20)?

_____

15. List three specific problems Paul noted among the Corinthians when they met to eat (v. 21). (1)_____

    (2) _____

    (3) _____

16. What did these faults imply about their attitude toward the church (v. 22)?_____

17. What did these faults indicate about their attitude toward the poor who had nothing (v. 22)? _____

18. From whom had Paul received instruction in these matters (v. 23)? _____

19. When did the Lord Jesus do the things Paul reported (v. 23)?

_____

20. What did Jesus say about the bread (v. 24)?_____

_____

21. At what time in the evening did Jesus take the cup (v. 25)?

_____

22. What did Jesus say about the cup (v. 25)?_____

_____

23. What does a Christian do every time he eats the bread and drinks the cup (v. 26)? _____

24. What terrible thing can be said of one who partakes of loaf and cup in an unworthy manner (v. 27)? _____

25. What should one do before he eats and drinks (v. 28)? _____

26. What happens when one eats and drinks unworthily (v. 29)?
_____

27. How should Christians treat each other when coming together
    to eat (v. 33)? _____

28. What should a hungry person do (v. 34)? _____

DISCUSSION QUESTIONS

1. How do you feel about Paul's opinions regarding the place of
   women in the church? To what extent was he pronouncing God's
   laws, and to what extent was he merely giving practical advice
   to help Christians solve their problems in Corinth? Have women
   today been harmed or helped by their struggles to live up to the
   image of the liberated woman?

2. To what extent should Christians be guided by what nature
   teaches us (v. 14)? If we were really guided by nature, would
   men shave? Would we wear clothes? Would we have such in-
   ventions as electricity, airplanes, telephones, explosives, and
   medicine? How can we decide when to follow the will of nature
   and when to seek to adapt nature to our own purposes?

3. What ordinances do you think Paul had given to the Corinthians (v. 2)? To what extent should Christians today practice
   them?

4. The instructions in regard to the Lord's Supper found in this
   chapter (vv. 20-33), are probably the oldest and most complete
   in all of the New Testament. On the basis of the discussion here,
   what would be your feelings about the questions below?
   (1) In what setting should the Lord's Supper be observed? During
       a meal? During a church worship service? At a home gather-
       ing?
   (2) How often should Christians observe the memorial feast?
   (3) What is the significance of the loaf? Of the cup?
   (4) Should the observance be for Christians only?

(5) To what extent should non-Christians participate in the service?

(6) How holy or righteous must a Christian be in order to partake? What makes him sufficiently righteous? What should be the attitude of a Christian participating in Communion?

(7) How may one commit the sin of eating or drinking in an unworthy manner? How can the Christian be sure that he is eating and drinking worthily?

(8) Who should officiate during the Communion observance? A minister? Elders? Deacons?

5. Jesus apparently taught His disciples that the cup of which they drank during the last supper signified a new covenant or agreement with God sealed with Jesus' blood. What is God's part of this agreement? What does He promise His people in this life? In the next? What does God expect of His people as their part of the covenant? In what ways is this covenant similar to God's agreement with Abraham? With Moses? In what ways is it different?

6. What did Paul mean by discerning or rightly judging the body (v. 29) as Christians eat and drink the Communion elements? Did he refer to the loaf and cup, to the assembly of Christians (the spiritual body of Christ), to the physical body of Christ, to the church universal? How do we properly discern the body when we eat and drink during the Communion observance?

1 Corinthians 12:1-31

CONTENT QUESTIONS

1. What topic did Paul announce for this chapter (v. 1)? _____

_____

2. If one said, "Jesus is the Lord," who inspired him (v. 3)? ____

_____

3. What was the range of gifts furnished by the one Spirit (v. 4)?

_____

4. For what purpose were people given manifestations of the Spirit (v. 7)? _____

5. List nine gifts of the Spirit (vv. 8-10).

(1)_____ (2)_____ (3) _____

(4)_____ (5)_____ (6) _____

(7)_____ (8)_____ (9) _____

6. Who made the decision about the distribution of these gifts (v. 11)? _____

7. What illustration did Paul use of the unity Christians have in Christ (v. 12)? _____

8. By what power were Christians baptized into the body of Christ (v. 13)? _____

9. In Paul's illustration, what reason did the foot give for its not wanting to belong to the body (v. 15)? _____

10. What reason did the ear give for its not wanting to belong to the body (v. 16)? _____

    _____

11. If the whole body were an eye, what problem would this body have (v. 17)? _____

12. If the whole body were an ear, what problem would this body have (v. 17)? _____

13. Who arranged the organs of the body (v. 18)? _____

14. How many bodies do these parts compose (v. 20)? _____

15. What could the eye not say (v. 21)? _____

16. What could the head not say to the feet (v. 21)? _____

    _____

17. What did Paul specify as our reaction to the parts of the body? How do we regard:
    (1) The parts which seem weaker (v. 22)? _____

    (2) The parts we consider less honorable (v. 23)?

    _____

    (3) The unpresentable or ugly parts (v. 23)?

    _____

18. If one member of the body suffers, what happens to the rest of the body (v. 26)? _____

19. If one member is honored, how do the other parts react (v. 26)? _____

20. Of what body are all Christians members (v. 27)? _____

21. List eight offices God established in the early church (v. 28).

    (1)_____ (2) _____

    (3)_____ (4) _____

    (5)_____ (6) _____

(7)_____ (8) _____

22. What questions did Paul raise about these various offices (vv. 29, 30)? _____

_____

23. What kinds of gifts should a Christian desire (v. 31)? _____

24. What did Paul promise to show his readers (v. 31)? _____

_____

DISCUSSION QUESTIONS

1. Paul said that special gifts of the Spirit were given to certain Christians for the common good (v. 7). What was the good accomplished by each gift? In Paul's day, what was the good of wisdom? Knowledge? Faith? Healing? Miracles? Prophecy? Distinguishing between spirits? Speaking in tongues? Interpreting tongues? Would these gifts be of any good to Christians today? Which ones? What would be the good?

2. Compare verse 3 with Matthew 7:21. What did Paul mean by saying "Jesus is the Lord" is an expression coming from the Holy Spirit? If it is said in the Spirit, why isn't the one who says it a member of the kingdom of God? Did Paul assume that the speaker would be sincere? What relationship with the Spirit does one need in order to say "Jesus is the Lord"?

3. How do you feel about miracle-working in the church today? Are miracles and healings genuine or merely applied psychology? Is there a distinction between miracles and answers to prayer? Do you feel that miracles are needed in the modern church? Can you imagine potential or actual harms? Would you personally like the ability to heal or to perform miracles? Why?

4. In this chapter, Paul clearly indicates that all Christians belong to the body of Christ even though some may have radically different gifts from the others. What essentials make one a Christian and distinguish him from the world? What do you think about expressions such as "born-again Christians, evangelical Christians, fundamentalist Christians, or New Testament Christians"? Are these terms accurate? Would Paul have approved of such

distinguishing names? Do they serve a useful purpose in our day? If so, what?

5. How well does the contemporary church measure up to the standard of Christian love Paul expressed in verse 26? Do we feel this way toward Christians in other countries? Of other races? Of other cultures? Of other economic classes? Of denominations? Do we hold to this standard within our own congregation?

6. Apparently the Corinthian church had many people with remarkable gifts of the Holy Spirit. How do you explain this fact in view of the many problems in that church? Does the Spirit give gifts to those who are not worthy? If the church had worthy members, why did it have such problems? Does the Spirit give gifts to counteract the effects of sin in a congregation? If so, why do we struggle to raise the level of our spiritual lives today? Do you think these gifts were present in Corinth in any particular way, or is the Corinthian church typical of all churches in this regard?

7. In what sense do Christians today have need of those who differ from them within the faith (see v. 21)? What is gained by our differences? Why is such variety important to us, to the communities to which we attempt to witness, to the church as a whole, to God's plan for the world? Can you think of any of these areas in which we do not need individual differences? At what point do you think differences may become harmful?

8. How do you explain the order of officers Paul indicated in verse 28? Why did he put apostles first? Why did he rank prophets ahead of teachers? Was he indicating an order of importance or a chronological order in which these offices came into existence? Would comparable offices have the same importance in the present-day church?

LESSON 13

1 Corinthians 13:1-13

CONTENT QUESTIONS

1. If I speak in any sort of language, but without love, what am I like (v. 1)? _____

2. If I have the spiritual gift of prophecy and have all knowledge, but lack love, how important am I (v. 2)? _____

3. If I have enough faith to move mountains, but lack love, how important am I (v. 2)? _____

4. If I give all my possessions to the poor, but without true love, what good will my giving do me (v. 3)? _____

5. If I give my body to be burned and die as a martyr, but without love, what good will my sacrifice do me (v. 3)? _____

6. Give two positive characteristics of love (v. 4).

   (1) _____

   (2) _____

7. Give three negative characteristics (v. 4). (Note that the verse division varies slightly in some translations.)

   (1) _____

   (2) _____

   (3) _____

8. List four more of these negative characteristics (v. 5).

   (1) _____

   (2) _____

(3) _____

(4) _____

9. What prevents love from being happy (v. 6)? _____

10. What makes love happy (v. 6)? _____

11. Give four characteristics of love which never change, under any circumstances, in regard to all other things (v. 7).

   Love _____ all things, _____ all things,

   _____ all things.

12. How permanent is love (v. 8)? _____

13. List three spiritual gifts which Paul considered temporary (v. 8). (1) _____

   (2) _____

   (3) _____

14. Which of these three did Paul expect to pass away because they were merely partial or fragmentary (v. 9)? _____

   _____

15. When did Paul expect these partial or fragmentary gifts to come to an end (v. 10)? _____

16. What three characteristics of childhood did Paul use to illustrate his point (v. 11)? (1) _____

   (2) _____

   (3) _____

17. When did he give up these childish ways (v. 11)? _____

   _____

18. What other ordinary human activity did Paul use to illustrate his point (v. 12)? _____

19. If Paul regarded his knowledge as partial when he wrote, how complete did he expect his knowledge to become in the future

(v. 12)? _____

20. What three qualities did Paul classify as abiding or permanent

(v. 13)? (1) _____

(2) _____

(3) _____

21. Of these, which did he consider greatest (v. 13)? _____

DISCUSSION QUESTIONS

1. Do you agree with Paul that love is more important than all the miraculous gifts of the Christians in Corinth? If so, in what sense is love so important? Isn't knowledge more basic than love, since you can't love someone until you know him? In what way would love be more important than faith and hope?

2. Define love. Notice that Paul's definition was essentially negative, listing the things that love is not (vv. 4-6).

3. What makes the difference between the kind of love Paul recommended in this chapter and the love we ordinarily experience in daily living? How can one tell the difference between love and chemistry when dealing with feelings for those of the opposite sex? How can true love for another person be distinguished from our own self-love? When we grieve because of the loss of a loved one, are we really sorry because of our love or because of the loneliness we will experience? Can we experience a love unmixed with selfishness? When?

4. Young people often ask, "How can I know when I am in love?" How would you answer this?

5. What did Paul mean by the perfect or "that which is perfect" (v. 10)? Do you think he had reference to a thing, a condition, a personality? Can you imagine any condition or situation prior to the end of the world which would make the gifts of tongues, prophesying, and knowledge unnecessary? What?

6. If love bears all things, believes all things, endures all things, is love blind? Why is love worthwhile if one has to bear all things and endure all things? Isn't it better never to love at all, if love involves pain and hurt? Wouldn't Jesus have avoided the cross if

He hadn't loved us? Would you agree that " 'Tis better to have loved and lost than never to have loved at all"? (Tennyson's *In Memoriam*)

7. In what sense are gifts such as knowledge, tongues, and prophecy to be regarded as childish? In what way are they like looking into a mirror rather than seeing reality? Why did Paul call them imperfect?

8. Should we expect to have gifts such as knowledge, tongues, and prophecy? If not, why not? If so, why are these gifts comparatively rare among Christians? How should a Christian go about trying to receive one of these gifts?

9. If love never fails (v. 8), how can God permit some people to go to Hell? Doesn't God love the whole world (John 3:16)? Then how can some persons be lost if God's perfect love never fails?

LESSON 14

1 Corinthians 14:1-40

CONTENT QUESTIONS

1. What should the Corinthians have taken as their basic aim or pursuit (v. 1)? _____

2. What one spiritual gift should they have desired (v. 1)?

   _____

3. If a man spoke in a tongue, to whom did he speak (v. 2)? __

4. If a man prophesied, to whom did he speak (v. 3)? _____

5. What was the exception that might cause speaking in tongues to be almost equal in importance to prophecy (v. 5)? _____

   _____

6. List three instruments Paul used as illustrations of the importance of clear communication (vv. 7, 8).

   (1) _____

   (2) _____

   (3) _____

7. If I don't know the meaning of a language spoken, how will the speaker regard me (v. 11)? _____

8. What should be the prayer of one speaking in tongues (v. 13)?

   _____

9. How did Paul pray and sing (v. 15)? _____

   _____

10. How effective was Paul at speaking in tongues (v. 18)? _____

11. What could possibly be better for Paul to do than to speak ten thousand words in a tongue (v. 19)? _____

_____

12. In what respect did Paul advise the Corinthians to be small children or babies (v. 20)? _____

13. For whom should tongues have been a sign (v. 22)? _____

_____

14. For whom should prophecy have been a sign (v. 22)? _____

_____

15. What might an outsider say if he heard a whole congregation speaking in tongues (v. 23)? _____

16. What would an outsider be expected to do and say if he heard a whole congregation prophesy (vv. 24, 25)? _____

_____

17. List five things early Christians had to contribute when the congregation assembled (v. 26). (1) _____

    (2) _____

    (3) _____

    (4) _____

    (5) _____

18. How many persons did Paul want to be permitted to speak in tongues during a service (v. 27)? _____

19. How many did Paul want speaking in tongues if no interpreter were present (v. 28)? _____

20. What principles did Paul recommend to govern the conduct of the service in which people wanted to speak in tongues or to prophesy (vv. 27-33)? _____

_____

21. What rule did he give women for speaking (v. 34)? _____

22. How should a woman learn anything (v. 35)? _____

23. What spiritual gift should the Corinthians desire (v. 39)? _____

24. What did Paul think should be done about those desiring to speak in tongues (v. 39)? _____

25. What general rule did he give for the conduct of a church service (v. 40)? _____

DISCUSSION QUESTIONS

1. Is there a place for speaking in tongues in the church today? Why or why not?

2. To what extent should Christian worship be emotional? To what extent should it be rational? Should emphasis be placed on things which give the worshiper the feeling of his being close to God and his fellow men? To those experiences of love and brotherhood? To a rational understanding of the great doctrines of the faith? How important are rational elements such as preaching, creeds, doctrines, offerings, and the like? How important are prayers, the observances of the Lord's Supper, singing?

3. To what extent should the Christian be rational in his witness to others? Can people be won to Christ by an appeal to the intellect or to the heart? How can these two be combined, and where should the emphasis be placed? What aspects of the usual church service would appeal to those outside Christ? Contrast 1 Corinthians 14:23 with 1 Corinthians 11:26. If Paul approved of the emotional, dramatic presentation of the death of Christ in the Communion observance, why did he object to the presentation in strange tongues?

4. What place should prophecy hold in the church today? To what extent would modern preaching be similar to prophecy in the

early church (note especially verse 3 of this chapter)? In what ways do you think modern preaching would be different? To what extent would our possession of the complete Bible make the gift of prophecy unnecessary?

5. To what extent should Christians participate in the leadership of the Christian assembly? Would Paul expect all Christians today to come to a church service with a hymn, a lesson, a revelation, a tongue, and an interpretation (v. 26), or should these things be left to ministers and choir directors? Wouldn't Christians bringing their own lessons result in all kinds of false doctrines? What do you think would be gained by greater participation in this way in our services? What might be lost?

6. What should be the position of women in the church service today? Was Paul stating basic Christian principles in verses 34, 35, or was this a command to suit local needs and problems? See Acts 21:9. How do you think Paul would have reacted to a church service in which Philip's daughters would prophesy? Do you think they spoke in a regular church service? Compare Romans 16:1, 2. If Paul expected women to have a passive role, why did he give Phoebe such authority? How do you explain Paul's commands to the Corinthian Christians in view of Phoebe's office in the nearby church at Cenchrea? Should women today teach in the Sunday school? Should they hold church offices? Should they be ordained as ministers?

LESSON 15

1 Corinthians 15:1-58

CONTENT QUESTIONS

1. Of what did Paul set out to remind the Corinthians in this chapter (v. 1)? _____

2. List the three great facts about the person of Christ which Paul had received (vv. 3, 4). (1) _____

   (2) _____

   (3) _____

3. What appearance of the risen Christ did Paul list first (v. 5)?

   _____

4. To whom did the risen Christ appear last, in Paul's listing (v. 8)? _____

5. Why did Paul consider himself unworthy to be called an apostle (v. 9)? _____

6. To what did Paul attribute his becoming the man he was (v. 10)? _____

7. What were some of the Corinthians saying about the resurrection (v. 12)? _____

8. What would have become vain or useless if Christ were not raised from the dead (v. 14)? _____

9. If Christ had not been raised, what would have happened to Christians who had died (vv. 17, 18)? _____

10. If Paul's Christian hope were for this life only, how would he feel (v. 19)? _____

11. What is the great historic fact of this case (v. 20)? _____

_____

12. Who will be raised from the dead when Christ comes (v. 23)?

_____

13. How long must Christ reign (v. 25)? _____

14. What will be the final enemy to be destroyed (v. 26)? _____

15. What reason did Paul give for the Son to be subjected, finally, to God (v. 28)? _____

16. What Christian practice demonstrated a belief in the resurrection (v. 29; compare Romans 6:3)? _____

17. If the dead are not raised, what did Paul recommend for our motto in living (v. 32)? _____

18. If his readers accepted the idea of the resurrection, what question did Paul expect them to raise (v. 35)? _____

_____

19. What illustration from ordinary life did Paul choose in order to try to answer this question (vv. 36-38)? _____

_____

20. What was Paul's second comparison in his answer (v. 39)? __

_____

21. His third comparison (vv. 40, 41)? _____

_____

22. Give the four great facts about the resurrection body which contrast with the body that was buried (vv. 42-44).

    (1) Sown_____ ; raised _____

    (2) Sown_____ ; raised _____

(3) Sown_____ ; raised _____

(4) Sown_____ ; raised _____

23. What mystery did Paul tell his readers (vv. 51, 52)? _____

_____

24. What is the saying that will come true when the mortal puts on immortality (v. 54)? _____

25. What is the real power of sin (v. 56)? _____

26. How should Christians behave, in view of the victory that is theirs (v. 58)? _____

_____

DISCUSSION QUESTIONS

1. The gospel is literally good news. In what respects would this gospel which Paul outlined be good news? How could it be called news? How could it be called good? Can you think of any other news you would regard as better? Why?

2. How valid was the evidence Paul presented for the resurrection? How reasonable was his case for his readers? How reasonable for us today? Can you think of other evidence that Paul did not include? Why did Paul place so much emphasis on proving the resurrection when it was only one aspect of the gospel? How does this one matter relate to the other parts of the gospel?

3. How valuable would the Christian faith be without the resurrection? Would you agree that without the resurrection we should eat and drink, for tomorrow we die (v. 32)? Isn't the Christian faith still valuable as a system of ethics without any belief in the hereafter?

4. What kind of body will a Christian have after the resurrection? How do you think Paul imagined the body he would have? How do you feel about your future existence? What kind of an existence do you think we will have in Heaven?

LESSON 16

1 Corinthians 16:1-24

CONTENT QUESTIONS

1. What was the first subject Paul discussed in this chapter (v. 1)? _____

2. On what day did Paul want offerings set aside (v. 2)? _____

3. Why did Paul want these offerings taken regularly before he got to Corinth (v. 2)? _____

4. What did Paul plan to do when he arrived in Corinth (v. 3)? _

_____

5. Who might also make the trip to Jerusalem besides the representatives from the Corinthian church (v. 4)? _____

6. Where did Paul intend to go before going to Corinth (v. 5)?

_____

7. How long did he intend to stay in Corinth (v. 6)? _____

8. How long did he intend to stay in Ephesus before leaving (v. 8)? _____

9. What two reasons did he give for remaining that long in Ephesus (v. 9)? (1) _____

   (2) _____

10. Whom should the Corinthians have expected to see before Paul (v. 10)? _____

11. What did Paul want them to do for this visitor (v. 11)? _____

12. What had Paul urged Apollos to do (v. 12)? _____

13. What advice did Paul give the Corinthians (vv. 13, 14)?_____

(1) _____

(2) _____

(3) _____

(4) _____

(5) _____

14. Who were the first Christian converts (firstfruits) in Achaia (v. 15)? _____

15. What were these converts doing (v. 15)? _____

16. What did Paul command of such people (v. 16)? _____

17. Name the three messengers from Corinth who had come to Paul (v. 17). (1) _____

(2) _____

(3) _____

18. What had they done for Paul (v. 18)? _____

19. Name two other individuals who sent greetings to Corinth (v. 19). _____ and _____

20. How did Paul expect Christians to greet each other (v. 20)?

21. Who wrote the greeting at the end of this letter (v. 21)?

22. What judgment did Paul pronounce on those not loving the Lord (v. 22)? _____

23. Give two things that Paul asked to be with the Corinthians (vv. 23, 24). (1) _____

(2) _____

DISCUSSION QUESTIONS

1. What should be the nature and purpose of the stewardship program in a church? To what extent is giving a part of worship? How much attention does giving deserve in the church service? Is there a danger that too much emphasis on giving will hurt the Christian witness to non-Christians?

2. How do you feel about giving a proportion of income, as Paul suggested (v. 2)? Should this proportion be a tenth or more? Is there a danger of our becoming legalistic about giving? How can we decide the nature of the income to be tithed? Gross or net income?

3. Why do you think Paul sent Timothy and Stephanas back to Corinth without sending Apollos? Do you think Paul was right in urging Apollos to return, or that Apollos was right in refusing to go? Is it possible for a church to have a minister who is too effective, too popular, too influential? What dangers do you see? What advantages?

4. How do you feel about a former minister's helping a church to solve its problems? Were the Corinthians doing the best thing in writing to Paul? Was Paul wise in answering their questions? Was he wise in planning to visit Corinth in person? Wouldn't the same arguments against the return of Apollos also apply to the return of Paul? What dangers do you see in Paul's return? Should a church today call a former minister to return and attempt to straighten out its difficulties?

5. To what extent was Paul lending his authority to Stephanas (v. 5)? What qualifications do you think Stephanas had for such leadership? How hearty was Paul's endorsement of Stephanas' leadership. How do you think the people in Corinth reacted to Stephanas as a leader? What dangers do you see in giving such responsibility to church leaders today? What advantages do you see in the procedure if it were followed today?

LESSON 17

2 Corinthians 1:1-24

CONTENT QUESTIONS

1. Who joined Paul in writing this letter (v. 1)? _____

2. To whom were they writing (v. 1)? _____

3. What two wishes did the authors express for their readers (v. 2)? (1) _____

   (2) _____

4. Give two attributes of God, the Father of Christ (v. 3).

   (1) _____

   (2) _____

5. What can be gained from God's comforting people in their affliction or tribulation (v. 4)? _____

   _____

6. In what two aspects of Christ's life did Paul believe he shared (v. 5)? _____ and _____

7. What did Paul feel would be the purpose of any affliction he suffered (v. 6)? _____

8. What was Paul's steadfast, unshaken hope for the Corinthians (v. 7)? _____

9. How badly had Paul been treated in the province of Asia (v. 8)? _____

10. What good had resulted from Paul's brush with death (v. 9)?

    _____

11. In view of past experience, what did Paul expect or hope that God would do for him in the future (v. 10)?_____

12. What sort of help did Paul expect from the Corinthians (v. 11)?

_____

13. What was the testimony of Paul's conscience, about which he felt he could be proud and happy (v. 12)? _____

_____

14. What was Paul's hope in regard to his earlier writing to Corinth, which they had read and understood (v. 13)?_____

_____

15. What reaction did Paul want the Corinthians to have toward him (v. 14)? _____

16. What schedule for future travel, including visits to Corinth, had Paul originally intended to follow (v. 16)?_____

_____

17. What request had Paul intended to make of the Corinthians in trying to carry out this schedule (v. 16)?_____

_____

18. What kind of person had Paul's enemies accused him of being because of his changes in plans (v. 17)? _____

19. Did Paul feel that this accusation was justified (v. 18)? _____

20. Who had been with Paul when he originally preached in Corinth (v. 19)? _____ and_____

21. How did Paul feel that Christ was related to the promises of God (v. 20)?_____

22. List four things that Paul felt God had done for him in his ministry (vv. 21, 22).

    (1) _____

(2) _____

(3) _____

(4) _____

23. Why had Paul refrained from visiting Corinth (v. 23)? _____

_____

24. How did Paul want the Corinthians to feel about their relations

with him, as they worked together (v. 24)? _____

DISCUSSION QUESTIONS

1. Paul indicated that one of the purposes in suffering is to be able to comfort others who suffer (vv. 3-7). Do you agree that one must have suffered in order to comfort adequately? Do you find this explanation sufficient to explain suffering? Can you think of other benefits accomplished by our suffering?

2. To what extent must our service to others depend upon first-hand, personal experience? Must we have suffered in order to comfort those who suffer? Must our suffering have been of the same kind? Must we have sinned in order to witness to the sinner? Are there cases where particular Christians cannot comfort or cannot witness because an inadequate background blocks their attempts to reach the other person?

3. If you had been praying for Paul in answer to his request, what would your prayer have been (v. 11)? What do you think Paul expected the Corinthians to ask of God for him? In view of what you know about Paul's subsequent life, what do you think he should have asked? Do we always know our greatest needs when we pray or when we ask for the prayers of others? Read James 4:2, 3. If you could have others praying for you about one thing, what would it be?

4. What did Paul mean by Christ's being the eternal yes of God (v. 19)? Do you think of Christianity as essentially affirmative or negative? Is one a Christian because of what he does or because of what he doesn't do? How do you think the average non-Christian perceives the Christian in this regard? How does the average Christian perceive himself?

LESSON 18

2 Corinthians 2:1-17

CONTENT QUESTIONS

1. Of what was Paul determined (v. 1)? _____

   _____

2. If Paul made them sorry, who would there be in Corinth to make Paul glad if he came (v. 2)? _____

3. Why had Paul written as he had (v. 3)? _____

   _____

4. In what mood had Paul written (v. 4)? _____

   _____

5. What had been his real purpose in writing (v. 4)? _____

   _____

6. Did Paul feel that the offender had been sufficiently punished (v. 6)? _____

7. Who had inflicted the punishment (v. 6)? _____

8. What did Paul feel that the Corinthians should do (v. 7)? ____

   _____

9. If the Corinthians didn't follow these instructions, what might result (v. 7)? _____

10. So what did Paul beg them to do (v. 8)? _____

11. What did Paul give as the reason for his writing (v. 9)? ____

    _____

12. How did Paul personally feel about the offender whom he wanted the Corinthians to forgive (v. 10)? _____

13. On what basis or for what reason was Paul so willing to forgive (vv. 10, 11)? _____

14. What one thing about Satan can we know (v. 11)? _____

15. What happened for Paul when he went to preach in Troas (v. 12)? _____

16. Who was missing in Troas (v. 13)? _____

17. Where did Paul go next (v. 13)? _____

18. What two things had God done for and through Paul (v. 14)?

(1) _____

(2) _____

19. What figure did Paul use to describe his work among those being saved and those perishing (v. 15)? _____

20. What was the difference in Paul's impact on the saved and the perishing (v. 16)? To one _____ ;

to the other _____ .

21. What did Paul deny in regard to his handling of the Word of God (v. 17)? _____

22. In whose sight did Paul and his companions speak (v. 17)?

_____

DISCUSSION QUESTIONS

1. Do you think Paul was right in asking the Corinthians to forgive the offender in their group? What information do you think Paul had? What kind of knowledge would he need to give such advice? Is this the kind of situation one can evaluate without actually being there? Why didn't Paul turn this judgment over to someone on the scene or wait until he could get to Corinth? Is it ever wise for us to offer advice at a distance?

2. How can we know when enough is enough? If one stops applying discipline too soon, will it lose its effect? If one continues
discipline too long and too harshly, will it cause a reaction? Do
you agree that the punishment should fit the crime? How can we
keep discipline from being too lenient or too excessive? In the
home? In the church? In society?

3. To whom does the Christian owe the duty of obedience (v. 9)?
Are there others whom the Christian is to obey (see Colossians
3:18-22)? Do Christians today have the same requirement of
obedience as did the Christians of the first century? How can we
obey the apostles today when the apostles no longer speak to
our problems? Isn't there a danger in our being too obedient,
that we may follow some leader into wrongdoing?

4. In what sense do things that pain one Christian pain all Christians (v. 5)? What causes such interrelationship? Are the church
fellowships you have known actually this close, or was Paul
describing an ideal we never really achieve? What do you think
or do that prevents us from finding this kind of fellowship?
Would we really be better off if we were this close to our
brothers and sisters in Christ? What may we do to make our
Christian fellowship closer and deeper?

5. Do we really want to be part of a fellowship in which we share
one another's joy and pain? What would be the disadvantages
of one's belonging to such a group? What would be the advantages? Do you think that non-Christians would find this kind of
fellowship appealing? Why?

6. Do you agree with Paul that we really know the schemes or
devices of Satan? Was Paul exaggerating to make a point?
What are some of the devices of Satan? If we know them, why
are we so easily tricked? What may we do to protect ourselves
against Satan's schemes?

LESSON 19

2 Corinthians 3:1-18

CONTENT QUESTIONS

1. State the two questions Paul used to begin this chapter (v. 1).

   (1) _____

   (2) _____

2. What did Paul have as a letter of recommendation (v. 2)? ___

   _____

3. Where was it written (v. 2)? _____

4. Who would read this letter (v. 2)? _____

5. With what kind of "ink" was it written (v. 3)? _____

6. Who made Paul sufficient or adequate for his ministry (v. 5)?

   _____

7. For what kind of work had Paul been qualified or made adequate (v. 6)? _____

8. What is the difference between a written code and the Spirit (v. 6)? The letter _____, but the spirit _____.

9. How splendid was the old dispensation in its coming (v. 7)?

   _____

10. How does the new dispensation of the Spirit compare in splendor (v. 8)? _____

11. What word did Paul use to describe the glorious old ministration or dispensation (v. 9)?_____

12. What word did Paul use to describe the glorious new ministration or dispensation (v. 9)? _____

13. What had happened to the splendor or glory of the old ministration (vv. 10, 11)? _____

14. What had caused this change in splendor or glory (v. 10)?

_____

15. How long did Paul expect the new dispensation or ministration to last (v. 11)? _____

16. How did this hope make Paul react in his speaking (v. 12)? _

_____

17. What did Moses do (v. 13)? _____

18. How did the Israelites react (v. 14)? _____

19. How did the Israelites in Paul's day react to the reading of Moses (v. 15)? _____

20. What happens when an Israelite turns to the Lord (v. 16)? _

_____

21. What exists where the Spirit of the Lord is (v. 17)? _____

22. What happens when one beholds or reflects the glory of the Lord with unveiled face (v. 18)? _____

DISCUSSION QUESTIONS

1. Why was Paul so critical of the laws of Moses? In what respects is our relationship with God in Christ so much more splendid than anything Israel knew under Moses? How would you convince an Israelite that life in Christ is better than life under the law?

2. In what sense does the letter kill while the Spirit gives life (v. 6)? Are there times when the rules must be spelled out? If laws are not explained in detail, how can they be taught and enforced? Aren't persons seeking freedom just hoping to find an excuse to avoid obedience to the law? Is it possible to teach children to live as Christians without first teaching them laws and rules?

3. If the average Christian is a letter of recommendation for his minister, on the basis of such letters what kind of ministry do we apparently have in our day? Do you think we speak and live as better recommendations than the Corinthians did for Paul? Wherein lies the fault that we are not better, in ourselves, in our ministers, or in the Holy Spirit? What changes should be made that we may represent a better recommendation?

4. What caused the minds of the Israelites to be hardened and veiled when Moses was read (v. 15)? What problems can you see in our day? What do you think may be done to remove this "veil"?

5. Why aren't more Christians changed into the likeness of the Lord (v. 18)? In what respects do we behold His glory? What influences prevent us from reflecting His glory? What is the Lord's responsibility to change us, and what is our responsibility to assist in working this change?

6. What would the world be like if a substantial number of people actually reflected the glory of the Lord? Would winning others to Christ become easier or harder? Why? What changes would take place in society? In law? In government? In our economic system? To what extent would sin be reduced? Would crime disappear because of the good example of the Christians? Would criminals have a field day with all the unsuspecting people to victimize?

LESSON 20

2 Corinthians 4:1-18

CONTENT QUESTIONS

1. Did Paul become discouraged or fainthearted as a result of his ministry (v. 1)? _____

2. What kind of activities did Paul renounce (v. 2)? _____

   _____

   _____

3. List two things Paul refused to do (v. 2).

   (1) _____

   (2) _____

4. How did Paul commend himself to every man's conscience (v. 2)? _____

5. To whom was Paul's gospel veiled or hidden (v. 3)? _____

   _____

6. Who had blinded the minds of unbelievers (v. 4)? _____

7. Why had he done this (v. 4)? _____

   _____

8. If Paul did not preach himself, whom did he preach (v. 5)?

   _____

9. In the beginning what did God do (v. 6)? _____

   _____

10. When God shines in human hearts, what kind of light does He

give (v. 6)? _____

11. What kind of container did Paul have for his treasure (v. 7)?

_____

12. What was the reason for such poor containers (v. 7)? _____

_____

13. Give four expressions Paul used to describe the problems he had been through (vv. 8, 9).

(1)_____ (2) _____

(3)_____ (4) _____

14. Why was Paul willing to submit his body to pain and danger similar to the death of Jesus (v. 10)? _____

_____

15. For whose sake was Paul willing to give himself up to death (v. 11)? _____

16. Where did he hope to have the life of Jesus expressed (v. 11)?

_____

17. What, then, was at work in Paul (v. 12)? _____

18. What did he hope was at work in the Corinthians (v. 12)?

_____

19. What did Paul's belief cause him to do (v. 13)? _____

20. List two things Paul expected the One who raised the Lord Jesus to do (v. 14). (1) _____

(2) _____

21. What did Paul expect to be the result of grace extended to more and more people (v. 15)? _____

22. What was happening to Paul's outer nature (v. 16)? _____

23. What was happening to Paul's inner nature (v. 16)? _____

24. What did Paul anticipate after the momentary afflictions of this life were past (v. 17)? _____

25. On what things did Paul have his attention fastened (v. 18)?

_____

26. Why did he concentrate on these things (v. 18)? _____

_____

DISCUSSION QUESTIONS

1. What blinds the minds of unbelievers to keep them from seeing the glory of Christ? Are they blinded by what they do or by the world around them? Do the actions of Christians ever serve to blind unbelievers? Are those things that blind their minds always evil? Are people sometimes blinded by things which are perfectly good in themselves?

2. What do you think about the god of this world (v. 4)? Is there an evil influence in the world outside the minds of people? How strong is this evil? What is its nature? Is it merely an influence or is it personal? Is Paul's language to be understood literally, or was he merely personifying forces which may affect people in the wrong ways?

3. Compare 2 Corinthians 4:1, 2 with 1 Corinthians 9:22, 23. What would Paul have been willing to do in order to save some of his listeners? What would he have refused to do?

4. Comment on each of the appeals given below. What truths do they contain? Do they also contain errors or half-truths? Would you change any of these appeals? Would you refuse to use any of them?
   (1) Salvation is a free gift. It won't cost you anything.
   (2) Accept Christ, and you won't have to worry about punishment for anything you've ever done.
   (3) Accept Christ, and you're sure to go to Heaven when you die.
   (4) Apply Christian principles in business, and you're sure to be a financial success.

(5) If you want all people to love you, simply pray for them and show them Christian love.

(6) Commit your home life to Christ, and He will make it a little heaven on earth.

(7) Weakness and disease are not in the will of God; Jesus heals every infirmity.

5. If God's power is best seen in our weakness (v. 7), why are Christians so eager to defend their own importance? What evidence can you see in the church today that Christians still maintain and enlarge their own egos? Isn't much of our worship, our church organization, our procedures with church groups designed to make people feel wanted, to make them feel important? Are such arrangements necessarily bad? Do we contradict ourselves when we work to make individuals feel important and then try to give the glory to Christ and not to ourselves?

6. Does the average Christian today really believe that Jesus was raised from the dead? In what sense? Is this belief a necessary part of the Christian faith? Does the average Christian really believe that he will personally rise from the dead? What is your own belief about life after death?

7. In what ways does God renew our inner nature every day (v. 16)? What experiences have you had which demonstrate this renewing? Do you think God renews us, whether we accept His power or not? What can we do to appropriate God's strength for our own lives?

LESSON 21

2 Corinthians 5:1-21

CONTENT QUESTIONS

1. If these early dwelling places of ours were to be destroyed, what would we have (v. 1)? _____

2. What did Paul regard as our natural feelings here (v. 2)? ___

   _____

3. What would be the result of our putting on and being clothed in our heavenly dwelling (v. 3)?_____

4. Why do we groan or sigh in this dwelling? What are we anxious about (v. 4)? _____

5. Whom has God given us, to assure us or guarantee us of our hope (v. 5)? _____

6. Should this frighten us (v. 6)? _____

7. What should we know (v. 6)?_____

8. How should we walk (v. 7)?_____

9. Where would we prefer to be (v. 8)? _____

10. Wherever we are, what should be our aim (v. 9)? _____

    _____

11. When we appear before the judgment seat of Christ, what will we receive (v. 10)? _____

12. Knowing the terror of the Lord, what should we do (v. 11)? _

    _____

13. Why did Paul want the Corinthians to be proud of him (v. 12)?

14. If Paul was beside himself, for whose sake was it (v. 13)?

15. If Paul was in his right mind, for whose sake was it (v. 13)?

16. What controlled Paul (v. 14)? _____

17. If one has died for all, what is the result (v. 14)? _____

18. Since Christ died for all, how should people live (v. 15)?

19. Whom did Paul no longer regard from a human viewpoint
(v. 16). _____

20. When one is in Christ, what is he like (v. 17)? _____

21. What had God done to bring all of this about (v. 18)?

    (1) _____

    (2) _____

22. What was God, in Christ, doing in the world (v. 19)? _____

23. What office did Paul hold (v. 20)? _____

24. What was Paul's message to the Corinthians (v. 20)? _____

25. What had God done to Christ (v. 21)? _____

DISCUSSION QUESTIONS

1. When Paul said that he longed to put on his heavenly dwelling
(vv. 2, 8) was he expressing an idea typical of Christians
today? Do most people live in eager anticipation of dying and
going to Heaven? If so, why do we work so hard to stay well

and keep healthy? If not, why do we find so much satisfaction in this life and anticipate so little our heavenly homes? Do you think Paul would have looked toward Heaven with less anticipation if his life had been less miserable?

2. Compare verses 10 and Romans 14:10 with John 5:24. Note that while John says Christians will not come into condemnation or judgment, Paul puts all people before the judgment seat. How do you explain this difference? What sort of judgment should Christians expect at the end of time? Who will be the judge? What will be the judgment relative to good or evil done in the body? What will be the rewards and punishments?

3. What would be the human point of view (v. 16) about Jesus Christ? How would Paul differ? What characteristics of Paul's view of Christ can you find in verses 16-21? Do you agree with all of these characteristics? Characterize your view of Christ.

4. How do we know that God had given us the Spirit as a guarantee of our immortality? Should the presence of the Spirit make us feel different in some respect? Review 1 Corinthians 12:8-10. Should we expect some manifestation of the Spirit in our lives by means of such gifts? Read Galatians 5:22, 23.

5. What do you understand by the ministry of reconciliation (v. 18)? What aspects of Paul's preaching and teaching pertained to this ministry? In what respects do you think Paul lived as an example of this ministry? To what extent are we concerned with this ministry today? In what specific ways can we teach reconciliation by word and by example?

6. Can we be reconciled to God without our first being reconciled to our fellowmen? See Matthew 5:23, 24. Can we really be reconciled to other people without being reconciled to God? Which should come first? As Christians what should be our primary message, for people to be reconciled to one another or to God?

7. If God has already reconciled us to himself in Christ (v. 18), why must we still be urged to be reconciled to God (v. 20)? Is any real change necessary, or did Paul merely intend for us to recognize what God has already done for us? Why was Paul still begging people to be reconciled to God? What did he want them to do?

LESSON 22

2 Corinthians 6:1-18

CONTENT QUESTIONS

1. What was Paul's entreaty to the Corinthians (v. 1)? _____

_____

2. What two things did Paul give as characteristic of that present

   moment in which he wrote (v. 2)? (1) _____

   (2) _____

3. Why had Paul put no offence or obstacle in anyone's way

   (v. 3)? _____

4. List several hardships Paul endured and by which he felt he
   could commend himself (vv. 4, 5).

   (1)_____ (2) _____

   (3)_____ (4) _____

   (5)_____ (6) _____

5. List several good qualities of which Paul was proud (vv. 6, 7).

   (1)_____ (2) _____

   (3)_____ (4) _____

   (5)_____ (6) _____

6. What weapons or armor did Paul possess (v. 7)? _____

7. List contrasting reputations Paul had with people in different

   places (v. 8). _____ and_____,

   _____ and _____

8. While Paul had been regarded as a deceiver or imposter,

what had he actually been (v. 8)? _____

9. Regarded as an unknown, what had he been (v. 9)? _____

10. Regarded as dying, what had he been (v. 9)? _____

11. Being punished, what had he successfully avoided (v. 9)?

_____

12. Regarded as sorrowful, what had been his real feelings (v. 10)? _____

13. Regarded as poor, what had he been able to do (v. 10)? ___

_____

14. Having nothing, what did he have (v. 10)? _____

15. How did Paul feel about the Corinthians (v. 11)? _____

_____

16. What did Paul ask of the Corinthians in return for his love for them (v. 13)? _____

17. List some things Paul felt would not mix (vv. 14-16):

    (1) Christians and _____

    (2) Righteousness and _____

    (3) Light and _____

    (4) Christ and _____

    (5) Believers and _____

    (6) The temple of God and_____

18. What kind of relationship should be between Christians and God (v. 16)?_____

19. What obligation does the Christian have as a result of this close relationship to God (v. 17)? _____

20. If the Christian fulfills this obligation, what will God do in return (vv. 17, 18)?_____

DISCUSSION QUESTIONS

1. How may one accept "the grace of God in vain" as Paul characterized it in verse 1? If one accepts the grace of God, how could that acceptance be in vain or empty? In what sense may one be receiving or accepting God's grace if it is to no purpose? Can you think of things which cause God's grace to be without purpose? What can we do, as Christians, to make certain that people do not receive the grace of God in vain?

2. Did Paul make a convincing case that he was a true fellow worker (v. 1) and servant (v. 4) of God? Which of his experiences would you consider the marks of God's true servant and which are merely bad fortune that anyone may suffer? If Christians today are also fellow workers with God, why aren't they going through the hardships Paul experienced?

3. Are Christians today generally regarded as critically as Paul thought they were in his day (see vv. 8-10)? Do people think of Christians as impostors, dying, punished, sorrowful, poor, having nothing? If not, is the change because we are less consecrated Christians or because we have done a better job of proving we are true, living, rejoicing, spiritually rich people who possess everything? Or have the times changed? How can we convince the world that we have all of these advantages when we seem to lack so much the world counts important?

4. Do you agree with Paul that many Christians, such as those in Corinth, need to widen their affections (v. 12)? What is the meaning of our having hearts or affections that are wide? What can individual Christians do to widen their hearts? How can a local church widen the affections of its members?

5. To what extent should Christians today be separated from the world? How can we sever ourselves from unbelievers and still live in society? How can we maintain our witness in the world while still being separate? Is too much separation a sign of exclusiveness which will offend people whom we are trying to win? How can we separate ourselves from people without sitting in judgment of them and their beliefs? In our confused religious world, is there a danger that any attempt to be separate will result in our cutting ourselves off from fellow Christians who happen to disagree with us on some points?

LESSON 23

2 Corinthians 7:1-16

CONTENT QUESTIONS

1. What should be the consequences of the promises Paul mentioned (v. 1)? _____

   _____

2. What was Paul's request of the Corinthians (v. 2)? _____

   _____

3. List three things Paul had refused to do in Corinth (v. 2).

   (1) _____

   (2) _____

   (3) _____

4. How close did Paul feel to the Corinthian people (v. 3)? _____

   _____

5. List four words or expressions which describe Paul's feelings toward the Corinthians (v. 4).

   (1)_____ (2) _____

   (3)_____ (4) _____

6. What had Paul experienced in his coming to Macedonia (v. 5)?

   _____

7. How had God comforted him (v. 6)? _____

8. What had Paul heard about the Corinthians (v. 7)? _____

   _____

9. What was Paul's reaction to what he heard (v. 7)?_____

10. What had been Paul's reaction when he wrote his previous letter (v. 8)? _____

11. Now how did he feel about his previous letter (v. 8)? _____

_____

12. What had been the Corinthians' reaction to his previous letter (v. 8)? _____

13. What reaction caused Paul so much joy (v. 9)? _____

_____

14. What may come from a godly grief (v. 10)? _____

15. What may come from a worldly grief (v. 10)? _____

16. Give several reactions produced in the Corinthians by their godly grief (v. 11). (1) _____

    (2) _____

    (3) _____

    (4) _____

    (5) _____

17. What was Paul's purpose in writing the previous letter (v. 12)?

_____

18. What had been Titus' reaction to the situation in Corinth (v. 13)? _____

19. What attitude had Paul expressed to Titus in regard to the Corinthians (v. 14)? _____

20. List two things Titus remembered about the Corinthians (v. 15).

    (1) _____

    (2) _____

21. Why did Paul rejoice (v. 16)? _____

_____

DISCUSSION QUESTIONS

1. How is it possible to reprove other people without giving offense? Recalling the first Corinthian letter, would you have expected the Corinthians to accept the criticism without becoming
angry? Why? Do you think the presence of Titus had anything to
do with the favorable reaction? What principles should govern
our attempts to correct others in the faith?

2. In the first Corinthian letter, who was the offender, the one who
did the wrong? Which sin mentioned in the earlier letter was the
worst? Which sin would involve one's doing wrong and another's
suffering wrong? In what way would the zeal of the Corinthian
church have been involved? Was Paul right in making such a sin
the business of the whole church? Why didn't he write or send a
messenger directly to the individual? (Note: The possibility exists
that this offender was mentioned in a lost letter and not in our
first Corinthian letter. What do you think?) Do we, today, tend to
handle such sins individually or as a congregation? Are we right
in our methods?

3. When Paul said he had been boasting to Titus about the Corinthians (v. 14), what do you think he had been boasting about?
From what you know about this church, what basis for boasting
do you see? Do you think Paul was really boasting about the
members or about some other aspect of the situation? What
aspects of your own church today do you think your minister
would have to boast about?

4. What problems did Paul face in Macedonia—the fighting without and fear within (v. 5)? Have you ever felt like this? Why does
God permit problems and temptations to strike us from the outside at our time of greatest weakness within?

5. What made Titus such a comfort to Paul (v. 6)? His news? His
personality? The situation in which Paul found himself at the
time? Are some people gifted with being able by their presence
to offer comfort and assurance? What qualities do they possess
which give rise to such comfort in those they meet? Can you think
of others who, by their presence, make people uncomfortable?
What causes this reaction? Is it best for a Christian to be one
who comforts the afflicted or one who afflicts the comfortable?

LESSON 24

2 Corinthians 8:1-24

CONTENT QUESTIONS

1. What did Paul want his readers to know (v. 1)? _____

_____

2. What had the Macedonian churches done (v. 2)? _____

_____

3. In what proportion had the Macedonian churches given (v. 3)?

_____

4. Who had persuaded the Macedonians to give (v. 3)? _____

5. What favor had these Christians asked of Paul (v. 4)? _____

_____

6. What had they given first, before giving money (v. 5)? _____

7. What instructions did Paul give to Titus (v. 6)? _____

_____

8. Give five ways in which the Corinthians excelled (v. 7).

(1)_____ (2)_____ (3) _____

_____ (4)_____ (5) _____

9. What did Paul want the Corinthians to prove (v. 8)? _____

_____

10. What did the Corinthians know about Jesus Christ (v. 9)? ___

_____

11. What advice did Paul give the Corinthians about this offering

(vv. 10, 11)? _____

12. Once the Corinthians were willing to give, what proportion would be acceptable from them (v. 12)? _____

13. How well off were the Corinthians when Paul wrote (v. 14)?

_____

14. What Scripture did Paul quote to emphasize his principle of equality (v. 15)? _____

_____

15. Who gave Titus his deep concern about the Corinthians (v. 16)?

_____

16. What did this concern motivate Titus to do (v. 17)? _____

17. How did Paul describe Titus' helper (v. 18)? _____

_____

18. Who had appointed this helper (v. 19)? _____

19. What did Paul want to avoid in the administration of the money he collected (v. 20)? _____

20. In whose sight did Paul want to appear honorable (v. 21)?

(1)_____ (2) _____

21. How did Paul describe the brother's helping in these matters (v. 22)?_____

22. How did Paul characterize Titus (v. 23)? _____

23. What did Paul want the Corinthians to prove (v. 24)?_____

_____

DISCUSSION QUESTIONS

1. What is the importance of one's giving self as well as offerings? Which is more important? Can one give anything without also giving something of himself? Do you think Paul would have accepted offerings from those who refused to give themselves as well? Should churches today accept pledges and offerings from non-Christians?

2. Why didn't Paul order the Corinthians to give? Should steward-ship be regarded as a command of the Lord as an essential part of the Christian life? Do you think Paul would have commanded giving if he had been writing to children new in the faith rather than to adults? If Paul did not want to make giving a command, why did he put so much pressure on the Corinthians to give generously? Is there a danger of over pressuring people so that they give as a matter of commandment rather than from a generous heart?

3. Why do you think Paul gave Titus the responsibility of the Corin-thian offering? Was it a wise move to let someone else finish a project he started? Was it really best for Titus? For the Corinthi-ans?

4. Why did Paul consider this collection to be such an important matter? To whom was it most important, to Paul, to those giving, or to those receiving? How important should collections be in the life of the present-day church? Does the average church put too much emphasis on giving? Too little?

5. Is giving necessary to prove that love is genuine? Can one love without giving? Is love any less genuine if one has nothing to give? If love is an inner emotion, why does it require outward expression? Is the emotion real whether it is expressed or not? Is it possible to give without love? In what sense does giving prove love?

6. To what extent should giving be proportional? Is it hard for the wealthy to give? Who receives the greater blessing from giving, the wealthy or the poor? Should the church ever refuse to accept gifts from those who are too poor to give? Suppose that the giving deprives a person of food, clothing, or the necessities for his family. Should such giving be forbidden? Why did Paul not mention tithing in this discussion?

7. In what sense is Jesus Christ an example for our giving? Paul mentioned only briefly the giving of Christ. What specific in-stances from the life and ministry of Christ should serve to moti-vate the giving of the Christian who names Jesus as Lord.

LESSON 25

2 Corinthians 9:1-15

CONTENT QUESTIONS

1. What did Paul consider superfluous (v. 1)? _____

   _____

2. What did he know about the Corinthians (v. 2)? _____

3. To whom was he boasting about the Corinthians (v. 2)? ____

   _____

4. What had Paul been saying about the Christians in Achaia
   (v. 2)? _____

5. What had been the result of the Corinthian zeal, emphasized
   by Paul's boasting (v. 2)? _____

6. Why was Paul sending the brethren to Corinth (v. 3)? _____

   _____

7. What might result if the Corinthians were not ready (v. 4)? __

   _____

8. In what spirit did Paul want the Corinthians to give (v. 5)?

   _____

9. What happens to one who sows sparingly (v. 6)? _____

10. What happens to one who sows bountifully (v. 6)? _____

11. Whom does God particularly love (v. 7)? _____

12. Through His abounding grace, what is God able to provide
    (v. 8)? _____

90

13. How does a godly person treat the poor (v. 9)? _____

14. List two things Paul expected God to do for the Corinthians, if they gave generously (v. 10).

    (1) _____

    (2) _____

15. What would the Corinthians' generosity cause or produce

    (v. 11)? _____

16. What would the rendering of this service by the Corinthians

    accomplish (v. 12)? _____

    _____

17. List two aspects of the actions Paul expected of the Corinthians which would result in glory given to God (v. 13).

    (1) _____

    (2) _____

18. What would the Christians who received these gifts be doing

    for the Corinthian Christians who had given (v. 14)? _____

19. Why did Paul give thanks to God (v. 15)? _____

DISCUSSION QUESTIONS

1. Was Paul wise in using the zeal of the Corinthian church (v. 2) to stir up the zeal of the Macedonians? Is it dangerous for a Christian to follow the example of another human? Should we fix our attention on Christ, following His example? What dangers can you see in following human examples? What advantages can you see? Are there situations which require human examples?

2. Is it wise for one Christian to boast about another (v. 3)? Which is better, to boast about or to criticize another person? Which situations call for compliments? For criticism? What should be our approach to young Christians? To mature Christians? Does it make any difference who offers the compliment or the criticism?

3. After all the pressure Paul put on them, do you think the Corinthians really gave willingly (v. 5)? What do you think the brethren

whom Paul sent would be doing? What would they say? Without undue pressure how could they raise a large offering? How is it possible, in any area of life, to get Christians to raise their standards of giving without forcing them or becoming legalistic?

4. In what sense does bountiful sowing lead to bountiful reaping (v. 6)? Is the reaping always in the same terms as the sowing? How can we convince people of this principle?

5. Since God is able to provide us with every blessing (v. 8), why doesn't He do it? How do you explain the problems of devout people who are poor or unhealthy?

6. What can we do to help people become cheerful givers? Is it natural for one to be cheerful in giving? How can cheerful giving be developed? What can parents do? Church leaders? Sunday-school teachers?

7. To what extent should thanksgiving depend upon the receiving of specific benefits (v. 12)? Do we wait until God give us something before we give thanks? Is thanksgiving our response to gifts, or is it as an attitude of mind?

8. Are words alone adequate for thanksgiving, or are specific deeds required? What are some of the means we can use to give thanks to God and to our fellows?

LESSON 26

2 Corinthians 10:1-18

CONTENT QUESTIONS

1. On what basis did Paul entreat the Corinthians (v. 1)? _____

_____

2. What sort of person did Paul seem to be, when present and when absent, according to sayings current in Corinth (v. 1)?

_____

3. What did Paul ask that he might avoid when he arrives in Corinth (v. 2)? _____

4. Describe Paul's warfare (v. 3). _____

5. What power did Paul's weapons have (v. 4)? _____

6. What did he expect to destroy (v. 5)? _____

_____

7. What did he expect to take captive (v. 5)? _____

_____

8. What did he expect to punish (v. 6)? _____

9. If a Corinthian were confident that he belonged to Christ, what should he keep in mind (v. 7)? _____

10. For what purpose had the Lord given Paul certain authority (v. 8)? _____

11. In his letter writing what impression did Paul want to avoid (v. 9)? _____

_____

12. What was the current saying about Paul's letters (v. 10)? ____

_____

13. About his physical presence (v. 10)? _____

_____

14. About his speaking (v. 10)? _____

15. How did Paul promise to act when he arrived in Corinth (v. 11)? _____

16. How did Paul's enemies prove their lack of wisdom or understanding (v. 12)? _____

17. How did Paul restrict his boasting (v. 13)? _____

18. What past accomplishment did Paul cite in support of his claims on the Corinthians (v. 14)? _____

19. What was Paul's hope for the faith of the Corinthians (v. 15)?

_____

20. What was Paul's ambition for his own work (v. 16)? _____

_____

21. What kind of boasting did Paul think was significant (v. 17)?

_____

22. What kind of commendation did Paul value (v. 18)? _____

_____

DISCUSSION QUESTIONS

1. What is the mood or tone of this chapter? Do you think it fits the earlier part of this letter? Do you find it harsh, as though written at some earlier time in Paul's dealings with the Corinthian Christians? Would this note have helped or hurt Paul's offering appeal in chapter 9? What situation in Corinth would justify the response Paul made in chapter 10? Should a minister today ever use an approach as strong as this one? Under what circumstances?

2. Which is easier, to deal with other people in person or by letter? Which is more effective? Which would you choose if you had to reprimand another person? What may have caused the reaction that Paul's bodily presence was weak? Would Paul have used the telephone in this case, had one been available? What advantages can you see in confronting people face to face? What disadvantages?

3. What were the weapons of Paul's warfare (v. 4; compare Ephesians 6:13-18)? In what sense could such weapons destroy strongholds? What strongholds would these be? How can we use these weapons effectively in working with other people? What factors prevent us from using these weapons effectively?

4. How can one be confident that he is Christian, that he is Christ's (v. 7)? On what basis should the Corinthians have recognized that Paul was Christ's and had authority in Christ? If one can't be certain of his own Christianity, how can he be certain of Paul's or of the Christianity of any other person? If the certainty of one's salvation depends on experience, how can anyone ever be certain of the faith of another? Did the Corinthians have any other basis than experience by which to evaluate Paul's faith?

5. Is it foolish for a person to compare himself with another (v. 12)? Did his claims of authority involve comparisons (v. 7)? Was Paul objecting to all comparisons or only to the standards of comparison being used by his critics? What advantages and what dangers can you see in one's drawing comparisons between persons—in the home, in the church, in the community? How can one draw comparisons without his being in danger of the sin of envy?

6. Was Paul right in his wanting to do Christian work in new fields without building on work done by others? Which do you think is easier, to begin a new work or to carry on one already started? What advantages do you see in each? What disadvantages? Which is more important to the ongoing of the gospel in our day? Should all Christians be expected to share Paul's views on this matter? What is your feeling about the kind of work God would have you do?

LESSON 27

2 Corinthians 11:1-33

CONTENT QUESTIONS

1. What did Paul wish his readers would do (v. 1)? _____

   _____

2. Why should Paul be jealous of the Corinthians (v. 2)?_____

   _____

3. Why did Paul think the Corinthians might be compared to Eve
   (v. 3)?_____

4. List three reports in which Paul feared that the Corinthians
   were easy to deceive (v. 4). (1) _____

   (2) _____

   (3) _____

5. In what quality did Paul consider himself superior (v. 6)?

   _____

6. In what respect might Paul have been unfair to the Corinthians
   and sinned against them (v. 7)? _____

   _____

7. While he was in Corinth how was Paul supported financially
   (v. 8)?_____

8. Who supplied Paul's needs (v. 9)?_____

9. Who knew Paul's true feelings about the Corinthians (v. 11)?

   _____

10. How did Paul feel about the false apostles (vv. 12, 13)? ____

_____

11. Whom were they imitating (vv. 14, 15)? _____

12. If the Corinthians would permit him some foolishness, what did Paul intend to do in this writing (v. 16)? _____

13. On what authority could Paul write this way (v. 17)? Not with

_____ , but as _____ .

14. What sarcastic reason did Paul give for his expecting the Corinthians to put up with some foolishness (v. 19)? _____

_____

15. What kind of treatment had the Corinthians been willing to accept from Paul's enemies (v. 20)? _____

_____

16. List four aspects of Paul's background of which he could boast (vv. 22, 23).

(1)_____ (2) _____

(3)_____ (4) _____

17. List four terrible experiences that Paul had undergone for the sake of his ministry (vv. 24, 25).

(1) _____

(2) _____

(3) _____

(4) _____

18. List Paul's eight perils (v. 26).

(1)_____ (2) _____

(3)_____ (4) _____

(5)_____ (6) _____

(7)_____ (8) _____

19. Through all of these experiences, what did Paul really worry about every day (vv. 28, 29)? _____

20. How did Paul escape from Damascus (vv. 32, 33)? _____

_____

DISCUSSION QUESTIONS

1. Was Paul correct in saying he robbed other churches (v. 8)? Was taking support from them to preach in Corinth really robbing them? Should the churches supporting Paul have felt that they were being robbed? What benefits can you see that they would have been receiving?

2. Do some people enjoy being put upon, that is, they like to have others take advantage of them (v. 20)? Isn't the Christian supposed to be inoffensive, to turn the other cheek when someone strikes him? Why did Paul criticize the Corinthians for doing what Christians are supposed to do? How are we supposed to know when to stand up for our rights and when to accept mistreatment without complaint?

3. How do you explain the suffering Paul endured? Wouldn't he have been better as a scholar in Jerusalem than as a missionary? What was his motive in going through such hardship? Couldn't he have served Christ in some way that called for less sacrifice? Are saintly people always called upon to suffer more than the rest? Why didn't God bless Paul in such a way that he would not have these trials?

4. Why was Paul so concerned for all the churches (vv. 28, 29)? Are all Christians expected to have a range of care and concern for another? How can this breadth of concern be developed today in our fellowship as Christians?

5. Why did Paul want to boast of things showing his weakness? What reason for boasting could he find in these things? Do Christians today have the same sense of values in this regard? Do we boast of things of which we should be ashamed? Are we ashamed of things of which we should boast? If our sense of values is twisted, what do we lack and where do we miss the standard Paul set?

LESSON 28

2 Corinthians 12:1-21

CONTENT QUESTIONS

1. What incident of his life became the subject of Paul's writing at this time (v. 1)? _____

2. How long previously did these events take place (v. 2)? _____

3. What happened to the individual about whom Paul was writing (v. 4)? _____

4. What was Paul's reaction to this incident (v. 5)? _____

5. Why didn't Paul tell more about some of these things (v. 6)?

   _____

6. What kept Paul from being too exalted about the incident (v. 7)? _____

7. Whose messenger was responsible for Paul's thorn (v. 7)?

   _____

8. What had Paul done about this affliction (v. 8)? _____

9. How many times had he done this (v. 8)? _____

10. What was God's response to Paul (v. 9)? _____

    _____

11. When did Paul feel he was strongest (v. 10)? _____

    _____

12. With what other important figures did Paul compare himself (v. 11)? _____

13. What evidence did Paul offer to support his apostolic authority
    in Corinth (v. 12)? (1) _____

    (2) _____

    (3) _____

14. What possible wrong had Paul done to the Corinthians (v. 13)?

    _____

15. How many times had Paul previously visited Corinth (v. 14)?

    _____

16. For whom was Paul willing to spend and be spent (v. 15)?

    _____

17. What basic question did Paul ask about the messengers he
    had used (v. 17)? _____

18. How did Paul refer to the person who accompanied Titus
    (v. 18)? _____

19. In what ways were Titus and Paul alike (v. 18)? _____

    _____

20. What was the purpose behind Paul's dealings with the Corin-
    thians (v. 19)? _____

21. What did Paul fear, in regard to his next visit to Corinth (v.
    20)? _____

22. What situation would cause Paul to mourn when he would
    arrive (v. 21)? _____

DISCUSSION QUESTIONS

1. How do you feel about the importance of unusual spiritual
   experiences in life? Are such things necessary for the Christian?
   Should they be a source of pride? Should they be discussed?
   Can they be the basis for a Christian witness? To what extent

does one's salvation depend upon such feelings and unusual experiences? Can you see any dangers in the repetition of such experiences? Why do you think Paul was prevented from telling the things he had seen and heard (v. 4)?

2. How should a Christian consider a physical handicap? Should he think of it as coming from God or Satan? Why does God permit suffering? Is a physical burden actually helpful in such cases? Can you think of other purposes that a handicap might serve? Is it right for us to ask to be delivered from such burdens? If our prayers are supposed to be answered, why wouldn't God answer this one? How should we react when God answers no to our prayers?

3. Is it ever proper for a Christian to boast? Is boasting an expression of the sin of pride? Are there circumstances in which boasting is all right? What are some of the dangers attached to boasting? What are some of the possible benefits?

4. In what sense can one be strong in weakness? Shouldn't we be ashamed of our weaknesses? Then how can they be sources of strength? To what extent should we reveal our weaknesses to one another? Is there a danger that the weakness of one person may lead another into sin? Is the concealing of weaknesses a form of hypocrisy? Are there some weaknesses which should be revealed and others concealed? Are there occasions when the discussion of weaknesses would be appropriate?

5. Are Christians today correct in accepting the authority of Paul and in studying his writings? To what extent do you think his teachings harmonize with the teachings of Jesus? Did Paul go too far in adapting Christian teaching to the Gentile world? Would a Jewish gospel have been more effective in the long run? What do you think of the criticism that Paul made Christian teachings too formal and institutional, that our real need is to go back to the simple, ethical teachings of Jesus?

6. In what respects was Paul like a parent to the Christians in Corinth? In what respects were they like his children? Were they childish? How would you define the maturity of their faith? Should this parent-child relationship also be true of church leaders today, of ministers and congregations, of missionaries and converts? Should one ever outgrow his child-like relationship to spiritual parents?

101

LESSON 29

2 Corinthians 13:1-14

CONTENT QUESTIONS

1. Paul planned to visit Corinth. How many visits would this make (v. 1)? _____

2. How many witnesses did the law require to confirm a point (v. 1)? _____

3. When had Paul previously given a warning to the Christians in Corinth (v. 2)? _____

4. What had been the nature of that warning (v. 2)? _____

   _____

5. Who was really speaking through Paul on this matter (v. 3)?

   _____

6. What earlier event had indicated Christ's human weakness (v. 4)? _____

7. By what power does Christ live (v. 4)? _____

8. What did Paul command the Corinthians to do (v. 5)? _____

   _____

9. If the Corinthians should pass the test, what would they discover about themselves (v. 5)? _____

10. What did Paul hope they would realize (v. 6)? _____

11. What did Paul pray for them (v. 7)? _____

12. How was Paul capable of acting in respect to truth (v. 8)?

13. What made Paul glad (v. 9)? _____

14. Name something else for which Paul prayed (v. 9). _____

15. What was Paul trying to avoid by writing this letter (v. 10)?

    _____

16. For what purpose had the Lord given Paul power or authority

    (v. 10)? _____

17. List four commands Paul gave in closing (v. 11).

    (1) _____

    (2) _____

    (3) _____

    (4) _____

18. Who would be with the Corinthians (v. 11)? _____

19. How were the Corinthians to greet one another (v. 12)? _____

    _____

20. Who else sent greetings (v. 13)? _____

21. List three things Paul hoped would abide with his readers (v.

    14). (1) _____

    (2) _____

    (3) _____

DISCUSSION QUESTIONS

1. What do you think Paul would have done had he returned to
   Corinth and found the Christians there disobedient to his instructions? Do you think he would have been forceful, or was he more
   powerful in writing than in person? How would he have brought
   the power of God to bear on such a situation? What procedures
   should be followed today when churches fall into the same
   errors which troubled the Corinthian church? Are there modern
   situations where strong action is required?

2. How did Paul expect the Corinthians to examine themselves to see if they were holding to their faith (v. 5)? What standards did they have for such an examination? What procedures did Paul expect them to follow? Is such self-examination still expected of Christians and churches today? Do standards and procedures differ in modern times?

3. Why did Paul feel it is impossible to do anything against the truth (v. 8)? Did he say this in reference to his own nature or to the nature of truth? What is the nature of truth? How is it possible to do anything against the truth? If an act against the truth is not possible, how would you explain falsehood? Did those who crucified Christ do something against the truth?

4. Is all divine power given for building up rather than tearing down (v. 10) or did this statement refer only to Paul's power? Can you think of situations where divine power is given for destruction? Isn't the best means of building sometimes to tear down, as in clearing the ground for the new construction? How can one who seeks to act in the power of God determine when he should be constructive and when destructive? How can we be sure we do not become destructive unintentionally?

5. What is the relationship of Jesus Christ, God, and the Holy Spirit? How can Jesus be Lord without interfering with our love and worship of God? Why did Paul identify grace with Christ, love with God, and fellowship with the Holy Spirit? In what sense was each term appropriately used? Why was it necessary for Paul to pray that these blessings should be with his readers. Aren't the grace of Christ, the love of God, and the fellowship of the Spirit always with us all?

6. What are your conclusions about the second Corinthian letter and the details of Paul's dealings with the Corinthian church? Do you find this letter complete in itself, or do you see parts of other letters here? What is your opinion about the various visits and events which resulted in these messages to Corinth?

7. What can you conclude about the personality of the apostle Paul? What was he like? Was he basically friendly or a disciplinarian? Would you classify him as broad- or narrow-minded? To what extent should ministers and evangelists today pattern themselves after Paul?